INVISIB

Frank Wright was bo ... ...
1922, and was educa... ...
School and St Peter's College, Oxford, where he
read Modern History. During the Second World
War he was a navigator in the Coastal Command
of the Royal Air Force, and after being shot
down in 1943 spent the rest of the war as a
prisoner in Stalag IVB in Germany.

He completed his Oxford studies after the war
and then went on to Westcott House, Cambridge, to train for the Anglican ministry.
Ordained in Durham Cathedral in 1949 he
served served curacies in Sunderland and Barnard Castle before becoming Rector of Stretford, Manchester, for eleven years.

Since then he has been: Canon Residentiary
of Manchester Cathedral (1966-74); Sub-Dean
(1972-74); Staff Tutor in the Extra-Mural Department and Honorary Lecturer in Pastoral
Theology in the University of Manchester
(1967-82). Since 1968 he has acted as religious
adviser to Granada Television. He is now Canon
Emeritus of Manchester Cathedral.

To Sir Denis Forman

Viro egregio
omni cultu et humanitate praedito
et semper hortanti

FRANK WRIGHT

INVISIBLE NETWORK
The Story of Air Care

Collins
FOUNT PAPERBACKS

First published in Great Britain by
Fount Paperbacks, London in 1989

Copyright © Frank Wright 1989

Printed and bound in Great Britain by
William Collins Sons & Co. Ltd, Glasgow

CONTENTS

PROLOGUE

~~~~

A Miracle of Synchronicity

> Whenever the hand of the distant past reaches out of its grave, it is always somehow absurd as well as amazing, and we tend to resist belief in it, for it seems rather magically to reveal some hidden order behind the amoral chaos of events as we rationally perceive them.[1]

On 3rd January 1988 I had such an experience, in which different elements in my past and present lives seemed to fuse together. On that Sunday morning, from the Granada studios in Manchester, we were transmitting over the ITV network, in the hour traditionally assigned to worship, the first of a series of three Meditations on the subject of Hope. I was presenting and exploring the theme, and made the commonplace point that in the grimmest of situations in which we find ourselves, we can often find small gleams of hope, tiny pinholes of light in the darkness. I then described something that happened forty-five years ago.

I told how one day, in the late summer of 1943, I was being marched by two German guards down a street in the Greek city of Salonika. I need to explain that six weeks previously my pilot and I, the navigator, in a twin-engined Coastal Command Beaufighter, had been shot down by anti-aircraft fire in a shipping strike on the harbour of Preveza, off the west coast of Greece. Since my pilot had been badly burned we had spent six weeks together in hospital, first in a casualty station in Preveza and then in a German military hospital in Jannina. We had then been separated, and I was being taken to a room in a large college building in Salonika where I was to be placed in solitary confinement – ironically, a building which during my stay there was bombed by the Americans. Small groups of Greek people were watching this strange spectacle of an English airman in shirt and shorts being marched along the street; in my disconsolate mood, I remember feeling cheered by the thought that most of them, however secretly, would be enthusiastic sympathizers with the Allied cause, and that thought was soon to be translated into a warm-hearted and generous action. A teenage Greek girl suddenly and most courageously stepped off the pavement and with a delightful smile handed me a bag of sweets. I described in the Meditation how that simple act of kindness lifted me temporarily out of my apparently hopeless situation, and gave me hope. I described how I could still remember the girl's face and her smile: such can be the lasting effect of goodness.

The transmission of the Meditations was followed by a pastoral care support scheme which we loosely called Air Care. It involved eighteen trained and voluntary counsellors responding to telephone calls from anywhere in the country. (Viewers could call at the price of a local call, Granada Television paying the difference.) The counsellors offered two resources: that of a listening ear to those who wished to tell out their troubles, and secondly, the possibility of a local personal contact, confidentially arranged, who would support them in their difficulties.

Of course, some viewers used the phones for other reasons: to voice their approval of the Meditations (or, very occasionally, their disapproval), or to ask questions about some material which had been used in the programme. One lady phoned to say that she came from Greece. She was staying with her daughter in London – curiously enough, during the three weeks in which our Meditations were being transmitted. Even more curiously, she said that she had been watching our programme on that morning when I recounted the incident which had taken place in Salonika forty-five years ago. She could (as she said later) hardly believe her ears, for she recognized that same teenage girl as herself, seventeen at the time, and now sixty-two. I phoned her at her daughter's home, and it was clear from our conversation, and from the dates involved, that we were almost certainly talking of the same incident – even though I could not for the life of me remember the details of the street down which I was being marched (including the Post Office at the corner!), all of which were so clear to her.

I still marvel at the coincidence and find it incredible. How could the lady be there at that particular time, watching that particular programme? It was a miracle of synchronicity. But more than that: it seemed to me to join together in a dramatic way many of the disjointed threads of my own life, and illustrate a continuity of which, until now, I had scarcely been aware.

CHAPTER ONE

~

The Music Hall Joke

You need to have a sense of humour if you are
born in or near the town of Wigan – "the joke", as
H. V. Morton, the travel-writer said, "that rocked a
thousand stalls". It wasn't that the town or its citi-
zens doesn't or don't possess solid virtues of a very
practical sort, let alone the continuing excellence of
its Rugby League team! It is the bemused sympathy
and condescension with which others receive the
news about your birthplace. (For a long time I
have been cheered by the question asked of Jesus's
home town, "Can any good come out of Nazareth?",
especially since Nazareth was in the north of a
small, obscure and despised provincial outpost of
the Roman Empire.)

Above all, you needed a strong sense of humour
and will to live through the Lancastrian depression
of the late nineteen-twenties and early nineteen-
thirties. George Orwell, of course, in *The Road to
Wigan Pier*,[1] portrayed something of the spirit of
that time, even though the people of Wigan have
found it difficult to forgive the way in which he
confused shabbiness with dirtiness. Poverty inevitably meant shabbiness, but the proud Lancastrian
housewife, scrubbing her doorstep with "Monkey
Brand" and "Donkey Stone", and polishing her front

door knocker with "Brasso", could never be accused of being dirty.

Such was the setting of my childhood: a cotton spinning factory at the end of the small road in which we lived, and mill girls in their shawls and clogs clattering up and down the road just before or after the blasting of the factory hooter. My father was a clerk in that same factory, and since he died suddenly when I was six, of what was then known as a heart attack, my memories of him are slight but vivid. One incident in particular stands out. Living in the same road two doors down was a boy called Noel, in the same class as myself at school. One Sunday, being taken for a walk by my father, we met Noel, and with the natural simplicity of a child I greeted him warmly – only to be rebuked by my father. "We don't speak to them", he said; not, I think, because there was any feud or quarrel between the families, but simply because, in a snobbish way, they were thought to be "different" from us. (They almost certainly had more money than we did, but somehow were "working class", in a way in which we were something different but unclassified.) That incident raised questions in my childhood mind which were perhaps the first faint stirrings of a concern for pastoral care. How could it possibly be that Noel was "different"? How could I possibly not speak to someone with whom I naturally played in the school yard? Could the God who (I was being taught) "loved us all", really want that? So shouldn't we all care for each other?

A year or two later I joined the church choir, and here I came into touch with one of the major influences in my life. (I was going to say "early

life", but how could I make that unreal distinction?)
The Vicar of the Parish of Upholland, four miles
from Wigan, was aristocratic to his fingertips, with
his double-barrelled name, his monocle, his public school and Oxford education, and his knighted
brother, the Governor of the Sudan. Few affinities of
background, you would think, with his Lancastrian
parishioners . . . But my first experience of that sort
of unconditional caring that the Church can offer
in its pastoral role came from him. I recall clearly
the soup kitchens he instituted on two days a week
for those of us who needed such nourishment; the
clothing vouchers which enabled me to have my first
pair of long trousers; the care of each one of us in his
confirmation preparation, even though my attention
at the time was rather more firmly fixed on Barbara,
in the girls' section across the aisle, than on any
growth in spirituality; the encouragement he gave
me to go to a summer school of the School of English
Church Music (now the Royal School), under the
redoubtable Sir Sidney Nicholson at Chislehurst in
Kent, a completely different world from Wigan —
and finally, when I dared mention to him my first
leanings towards ordination, his profound wisdom,
a subtle blend of encouragement and realism. His
example of unconditional caring has remained an
inspiration for me throughout my life.

But there was another inspiration, too. The small
co-educational grammar school I attended and which
was my launching pad for University, wasn't a school
renowned for its Oxbridge scholarships. Two only
had occurred in my time there. I had an uncle by
marriage who, having given up the Headmastership
of this same grammar school at the age of sixty-five,

was ordained and became Rector of an idyllic parish twelve miles from Oxford. The Rectory was enchanting, with a stream running through the garden, big enough to allow for a small punt, and a waterfall, ideal for splashing about in like baby elephants. I spent many happy hours of my summer holidays there; and my lovable, distracted and neurotic aunt (my father's sister) insisted, as she took me into the city of Oxford, wearing a straw hat much too large for me, that one day I would come to that University. That ambition would never have been realized had it not been for the care and hard work lavished on two of us in the Sixth Form by our history master, who first awoke in me a genuine thirst for reading and learning. Until then, there was little in my school work that enthused me; I was far more interested in cricket and rugby, not to mention the local cinema when pocket-money would allow. It was the history master's belief in our potential (always a characteristic of good pastoral care), and his availability and willingness to give up his own free time (additional qualities of such care), which more than anything else ensured a place for my friend at Cambridge and for me at Oxford.

There were literary and philosophical experiences, too. I remember a not very intelligent boy in the Fourth Form coming in to the classroom one morning and telling me that the previous night he had been reading a novel by an author (sadly, almost forgotten today) called Charles Morgan. He gave me to understand that it was exciting stuff, not least because of its love interest! That sparked off my enthusiasm, and I became absorbed in two of his earliest novels, *The Fountain* and *Sparkenbroke*.[2] In retrospect, it

was Charles Morgan's insistence on the quest for
personal identity, the importance of relationships,
and the necessity to embark on a personal "voyage"
which helped to affirm my growing conviction about
the concerns of personal and pastoral care. And what
Charles Morgan hinted at in his novels, I found
explicated in the writings of John MacMurray, the
philosopher. It was his book *Reason and Emotion*[3]
which opened my questioning eyes more than any
other, and his insistence that "persons are consti-
tuted by their mutual relations to one another"
again deepened my conviction about the over-
riding importance of pastoral care.

Looking back on my childhood and youth, then,
it is clear that several influences from very different
quarters, and not least the quiet self-sacrifice of a
very unpious mother, were combining to form in
me the realization of the importance of the simple
business of caring. Its results seem to be incalculable.
Of course, despite my leaning towards ordination, I
did not restrict this caring to the Church and – apart
from those like the Vicar, who were an essential part
of it – had not yet come to see the direct connection
between the unconditional love of God and unconditional pastoral caring. Indeed, not only were the
nineteen-thirties not the most creative period in the
history of the Church of England (to say the least),
but my interest in the Church at that time was largely a musical interest, since I progressed directly and
rather unusually from singing treble to singing alto.
As to the other activities of the Church, I felt slightly
superior towards them, especially in the Sixth Form,
when life was interesting enough with many other
pursuits, let alone working hard to get to University.

I arrived there in October 1940, and on the night of my arrival was confronted by a small and earnest group of Evangelicals, who wished, as they said, to make me their "target for tonight" at the "coffee squash" to which I was invited. "Target for tonight" was beginning to be a common phrase in an era of bombing, and was the name of a film describing a bombing mission. It wasn't, I think, simply the stubborn obstinacy in my character which made me react in a quite contrary direction to the Evangelical appeal. My already half-formed belief was that the salvation of my own soul ought not to be my chief religious concern: the Christian faith was essentially about losing even that concern for the sake of others, giving pride of place to a love of neighbour, which involves caring for all. Soon, that half-formed belief was to face a still sterner test.

CHAPTER TWO

Wartime Oxford

1940-41 was a strange, disjointed time to be up at Oxford. There were nine months of an academic year to go through, Part One of a Modern History syllabus to be examined in, and one-and-a-half days a week at the University Air Squadron doing basic training. Although I had been accepted as an ordination candidate in the Liverpool Diocese in 1938, I realize now that I became detached from and almost a spectator in the life of the local church. I would go to church in the vacation, but I felt slightly superior in my long green, blue and yellow college scarf, my pipe largely unsmoked but visible for all to see as a symbol of my virility – and I remember how quaint and irrelevant the Church seemed in days when France and the Low Countries had fallen to the Germans, and we couldn't see how we could even begin to turn the tide.

Soon I was to have another personal reason for disillusionment with the Church. In addition to what I had secured by way of scholarships and bursaries to go to Oxford, I still needed £50 to cover my costs for the year from an outside source, since my mother was obviously unable to help me financially. What more natural than that I should turn to the Church, whose ordination candidate I was? After all, I felt,

I had done a lot through my own efforts in working hard. Surely the Church could recognize me to the tune of £50? So, on the advice of the new Vicar of Upholland, a Mirfield-trained priest, I applied first to the Anglo-Catholic Ordination Candidates' Fund. I remember going up to London for a bizarre interview at Westminster with some black-coated priests in a small office. I soon realized what a big stumbling block there was in the way of my being given a grant, for I was asked which college I was going to in Oxford, and when I breathed the words "St Peter's Hall", it was as if I had uttered a blasphemy. For St Peter's Hall had been specifically founded by Bishop Chavasse as an Evangelical college, and there was no way in which the Anglo-Catholics were going to subsidize a student at an Evangelical foundation. So what more natural again than that I should now apply to the Evangelical Ordination Candidates' Fund? My Oxford college surely had impeccable credentials in that respect. But again, my hopes were to be dashed, for as soon as I was interviewed it was clear from what I had said about my own church background that I wasn't "sound" evangelically, and consequently not worthy of help.

Looking back from this distance of nearly fifty years, I wonder now that my faith was strong enough to surmount such partisanship and bigotry. In the end, it wasn't the Church at all which came to my rescue, but a secular educational Trust founded by Sir Richard Stapley (I know nothing about him, but I bless his name!) which saw me through. Had it not been for such secular help, the Church would inevitably have lost me as an ordination candidate.

In a sense, however, it wasn't the Church that

mattered at that time. I can't think of a single point at which, at this vital time both in the world's history and in my own personal history, the Church as the Body of Christ made a significant impact on my life – the sacraments, of course, apart. What did matter was Christian faith and its defence, when obviously questions like "Why did God allow the war to happen?" were being hurled at it. Here, C. S. Lewis was proving a tower of strength with his confident and combative assertiveness about the truth of the faith, his neat certainties about what was right and what was wrong. Recently, I have come to see the importance of C. S. Lewis rather differently, consequent upon what happened later on in his life.[1] But at the time his influence was immensely encouraging, and I still remember the thrill of seeing him in his tweeds and corduroys, pipe at the ready, and hearing him defend his faith at a meeting of the University Socratic Society. Today, the relentless exposure to evil in the world, from which we all suffer, seems to present powerful emotional arguments against the truth of the Christian faith, and the counter-arguments advanced are not so much intellectual but to do with the validity of the struggle to hold on to faith, almost by one's fingernails. It is Job's cry, "Though He slay me, yet will I trust Him" transposed into late twentieth-century terms.

During the war, my impression of what mattered was the triumph of the rational arguments, despite all that was happening in the world – and here C. S. Lewis was of supreme importance. He represented some sort of thread on which my faith hung, for, as I say, the feelings of being part of a warm, caring community, and of being supported through all the confusions of the time, were almost completely absent. The nearest I got to it, I suppose, was sitting in the crowded gallery in those 8 p.m. Sunday evening services in the University Church of St Mary's, but there again the appeal was an appeal to the mind as a well-known preacher justified the ways of God to man in a half-hour address.

Was I expecting too much? Facing the exciting uncertainty of the next few years, I found stronger comfort in the poems of Wilfred Owen and Rupert Brooke and the like than in anything which the Church had to offer. In retrospect, I can see that this vacuum, this very blankness, was forming in me certain convictions about the Church and what the Church should be. I had read several little books about the Church as the Divine Society, the extension of the Incarnation, the supreme Body of Christ on earth. But where were the golden marks of that Divine Society to be seen and experienced – locally? Apart from the lives of some individuals within it, I saw little evidence of a society that was giving itself away for the sake of God and other people.

CHAPTER THREE

In the Bag

Two months after completing the History Part One examination, in August 1941 I found myself in the Royal Air Force, with little time (or indeed inclination) for theological speculation. For the next four years I was due to spend only five months in Britain — and nearly all of that in Scotland. A month at the Royal Canadian Air Force Base at Sunnyside in Toronto, four months in Miami, Florida, doing Astro-Navigation training at Pan American Airways, operations-training in Prestwick, East Fortune and Charter Hall — and then out to the Middle East and to 252 Beaufighter Squadron of Coastal Command. Our Squadron, from different aerodromes along the Mediterranean coastline, was to protect our own shipping from air attack, and to make offensive air strikes on enemy shipping and other targets. Of the Church at that time there was little to tell: occasional visits with American friends to the fashionable Episcopal Church in Miami, Christmas Eve midnight communion in Cairo Cathedral — but I recall only one fleeting visit from a Chaplain to our Squadron, and that in a purely formal sense. (I have to confess that, if such an adjective had been in vogue then, I would have described him as rather wet.)

The impulse which really sustained me then was

not so much religious as humanitarian: the thought that we were fighting the war to get rid of the Nazi evil. After all, that was what motivated me to join the Air Force in the first place rather than embracing pacifism, since I thought (mistakenly?) that by comparison war was the lesser of the two evils. Once the war was out of the way, I imagined, we could begin to build a more just social order than that of the squalor and poverty which I had seen in the Lancastrian depression ten to fifteen years earlier. I recall that in the glossy Miami Cadets' Course magazine, which contained a photograph, biographical note and comment from each one of us, I rather pompously made some remark to that effect – but of course what I really wanted was to get the war over, get back to Oxford as quickly as possible, and resume a life of normality. I was encouraged in my better moments by the yellow books published by the socialist Victor Gollancz, and by the speeches and writings of Archbishop William Temple, especially his *Christianity and the Social Order*.[1] A mood of cynicism had begun to take over as the war dragged on, and not long ago an Oxford friend of mine handed me back a letter full of self-pity and bitterness which I had written to him from our desert base, about six weeks before being shot down.

It happened at noon on Sunday 22nd August 1943. Three aircraft, of which we were number two, had taken off from Benghazi to attack a ship in Preveza Harbour. Only number one returned. Whilst we were in the water, we saw that number three had crashed on land, and both pilot and navigator, we discovered later, had been burnt to death. Our port engine had been set alight by anti-aircraft fire, and mercifully my pilot had the presence of mind to ditch the aircraft; otherwise, we should have suffered the same fate as number three. So there we were: two dripping figures in the sea, my pilot in considerable pain from the effect of salt water on the extensive burns to his face and arms, and both being hauled aboard two speedboats with rifles pointed at us. We landed at the harbour in Preveza, watched by a curious crowd, for whom the whole event had obviously been quite a Sunday morning entertainment. Taken to the casualty station, we were made to wait for nearly three hours before treatment could start, while the crew on board the ship which had been our target and whom we had wounded with our cannon shells, were treated first. Their cries and screams I can still hear, like a piercing and ringing judgement on the beastliness of war.

All the deceptive glamour surrounding the image of Royal Air Force air crew (the "Brylcreem Boys") was put into perspective in those moments. We now *knew* war, in a way in which, flying over the waves at fifty feet, hitting targets and then flying back again, it had always been hidden from us. Taken to hospital, we battled for my pilot's life, and then removed to Salonika and the Greek girl's sweets . . .

From Salonika, I was flown up to Austria in a German military transport plane (a slow Junkers 52, several of which our Beaufighters had shot down, a fact which did not exactly inspire my confidence). Landing in Vienna, by now in late October, I realized what a strange sight I must have looked, still clad in shirt and shorts, accompanied, of course, by the German guard, and clutching some bread and

German sausage as my only precious possessions. I was taken by train to Frankfurt and another spell of solitary confinement and interrogation.

I have read accounts of how other prisoners spent their time in such confinement, often much longer than my spell of twelve days and in far worse conditions, very often under the threat of torture; and I have read, too, of the way in which their faith sustained them, through reading the Bible and through an earnest prayer life. Mine is a much humbler story, of a certain resource of spirit, allied perhaps to a natural obstinacy (which, I have to say, stood me in good stead during the course of my interrogations) and a sort of bottom-line faith that in the end "it would be all right". (Perhaps that is the secularized version of St Paul's statement in the eighth chapter of his Letter to the Romans, that "nothing shall separate us from the love of God".) I had no sense of the beloved community of the Church being alongside me, although doubtless certain individuals were praying for me, and some told me so afterwards. My mother, incidentally, had every reason to believe I was dead, since I had been reported "missing, believed killed", and it was as long as six months after being shot down that any word got through to her that I was safe.

The journey from Frankfurt to Muhlberg in Saxony, the site of our camp (IV B) for the next eighteen months, was in the legendary cattle trucks, with thirty or so of us sitting or lying on the floor of the truck. On our arrival at the camp we all had our heads completely shaved, the quickest haircut I have had in my life!

There were, to our surprise, four padres in the

camp, two Church of England, one Free Church and one Roman Catholic, all of whom had been taken prisoner in Italy and transferred to Germany, and although very different from each other, they had a quality about them of which the Church might well be proud. We were able to have some church services in the recreation hut – until the Germans discovered that a tunnel had been started beneath it! There was a time when our four padres were removed from camp for some unexplained disciplinary reason, and several of us on the "Church Committee" took over the organizing of church services – even, I recall, the preparation of some confirmation candidates, although I dread to contemplate the quality of that preparation! Again, it is interesting to remember that it was the church services that mattered: I don't think we ever agonized over what, as a little community within that massive collection of human- ity, we might be doing in terms of "giving ourselves away" for its sake. True, we often had difficulty in surviving ourselves – especially towards the end of the war when food was scarce and no Red Cross parcels arrived, because of the way in which our bombing had dislocated German transport. But in camp, as too often elsewhere, the Church proved to be a hobby and diversion for those who liked that sort of thing, even an escape from a harsh world of reality, rather than a resource which might in some way service those upon whom that harsh world was impinging most. I freely admit that it is difficult to see how it could have been done, but it is very sig- nificant that we never even asked the question.

The lasting value of POW experience for me was twofold; first, I learnt to "make" life with no tools at all. It was an important lesson in recognizing the inner resources you possessed to cope with any situation, and respond creatively. Secondly, you experience the heights of courage and nobility to which men can rise in desperate circumstances – and the depths of cut-throat selfishness and near-bestiality to which in similar circumstances they can also descend. (I was going to write "men and women" in the last sentence, and of course the same would be true of both, but since our only contact with members of the opposite sex in camp was through spasmodic letters or from one glimpse of some temporary Polish women prisoners in a camp thirty yards away, I can hardly include them!)

Release came in April 1945, when four Russian cavalrymen rode down the main street in the camp, most of our German guards having disappeared overnight, and soon it became a matter of escaping from the Russians, since, having marched us to another camp at Riesa twenty miles away, they showed no signs of handing us over. In small groups, sometimes two by two, we made our way back to the American lines, and so to freedom . . .

By the middle of October that year, 1945, I was back at Oxford, starting to work on two more years of history to complete my degree, before going off to theological college. It soon dawned on me, however, that there was a difficulty. Naturally, I had gone back to church at home in Oxford, and was fairly disillusioned by what I met. With the life-and-death experiences of the war still vivid in my memory, it was difficult to believe (and I will grant it was an emotional rather than a rational protest) that the Church had not moved one

iota during my absence, and did not seem to be
responding with any great realism or relevance to
the deep needs of the people around it. It seemed
to be stuck, if anything even more firmly, where it
had been in the nineteen-thirties. Was this the Body
to which I wanted to commit myself for life? Could
a parish church ever respond to those deep needs?
There seemed to be little inspiration towards such
commitment, and little evidence that parishes were
capable of rising to such a level.

All the emphasis seemed to turn inwards, towards
the importance of the domestic life of the Church,
rather than what I saw to be of its essence: the
losing of itself to find itself. No, I thought; it
can't be for me. So what could I, what should I,
do in life? History fascinated me, and the prospect
of teaching adults was exciting. So off I went to
Rewley House, the home of the Oxford University
Extra-Mural Delegacy, to offer myself for a possible
appointment.

But the Hound of Heaven (or something like
it!) wasn't going to let me get away so lightly.
Sitting up far into the night with several friends,
one or two of whom had had prisoner-of-war camp
experience, but in different camps, the discussion
went backwards and forwards. What were we really
about but to change things? Why had we gone into
the war at all, but in order that we should see the old
order die, and be midwives to the new? If the Church
were part of that old order, and yet the Christian faith
were true, shouldn't the Church be changed? And
who should help to do that, but us? That was an
appeal to my pride and big-headedness, if ever there
were one, but then, I did not need to be convinced in

a post-Freudian age about the mixed motivation that leads us all in the direction of ordination, or indeed to any other altruistic cause! There was only one way forward: I applied for entrance to theological college at Westcott House, Cambridge, and my feet seemed fairly well set in the direction of ordination. "There is nothing sweeter than the smell of burning boats", as a dear friend used to say – so there was a very sweet smell around . . .

All my experience of life up to this point had taught me what I wanted to see in and from the Church. I primarily wanted it to take its pastoral role seriously. It seemed to me that it was far too prone to let matters of ecclesiastical organization take over and dominate things, and that its care for people was both tainted and spasmodic. It was plain and obvious from living at such close quarters with 279 other men in a barrack-block, that for the vast majority the Church did not touch their lives at any significant point whatsoever. It was not a matter of "changing the language" (the "new services" have exploded the myth that the antiquated liturgical language is the principal barrier to religious commitment); it was a matter of touching them with the quality of life and care that could not be found anywhere else. Church people often complain that those outside the Church only want it at the point of "hatches, matches and dispatches", but this should say something to us about the way in which these rites of passage are seen to be relevant at the deepest and most intimate moments of a person's life: at the moment of childbirth, commitment in marriage, and at the death of a loved one. If at these points people dimly perceive some need, why not at others? They have never, in other words, experienced the church in such an unconditional, caring role in the ordinary areas and affairs of their lives that they have been prompted to make a response. Could a parish church do this?

I was soon to find out.

CHAPTER FOUR

The Church, At Last

Large parish churches in the earlier years of this century tended to work on the "octopus theory". You provided a number of different clubs and organizations designed to meet the social needs of as many different groups as possible; some tentacles of the octopus would then "touch" especially those who would not be likely otherwise to set foot inside the church, and consequently bring them into the fold. In days before leisure pursuits became as sophisticated as they are now, and before teenagers enjoyed the more affluent lifestyle they do today, this was a valuable piece of social service. As someone put it, the church provided table-tennis tables for young people, billiard-tables for working-class men, and tea-tables for the ladies. But a huge question mark hung over that word "touch". How were people to be "touched"? Was there to be any insistence on some minimal church attendance in order to be able to join these clubs? Was the epilogue at the end of each youth club evening to be compulsory or not? In other words, was the church to be an open or closed society, or was it to be an uneasy compromise between the two?

I soon saw the relevance of this question after my ordination in Durham Cathedral in June 1949, to serve in a parish in the centre of Sunderland with a Rector for whom I have the greatest affection and respect, and who believed very strongly in the "octopus theory". One of the tentacles of our particular octopus was a boys' club, many of the boys being shipyard apprentices. It had the usual games facilities, and a soccer team which took itself very seriously, and saw itself as a "nursery" through which to provide players for professional clubs like Sunderland itself – at that time in the First Division! I had no evidence, but I always suspected that our over-zealous manager of the team and secretary of the club attracted boys to become members of the club through a half-promise of such a possibility.

We had an annual camp when twenty or so of us spent a happy week camping at Knitsley, near Consett. And some of my most unusual and happy experiences of celebrating Holy Communion have been at that camp, celebrating in the open air and using a small tree trunk for an altar. There was no compulsion to attend, and in any case no more than six or seven of the boys were confirmed, so there was a small congregation – but there lay the rub. The most that was expected of the boys religiously was that they should come to Matins once a month on the Sunday when the other uniformed youth organizations attended. No one was expelled for not coming, but a certain amount of pressure was brought to bear on the boys, more particularly by the chairman and the secretary, since they both thought that it was well to "keep in with the church" . . . I could never bring myself to exert such pressure, and was always uneasy about it; were we not being guilty of what could easily be considered as bribery?

Further, the incongruity to be observed every time some of the boys came to Matins on Sundays other than the "youth Sunday" was acute. Gathered at the back of the church in some side pews, far removed from the rest of the congregation, what sort of sense would any of them be making of the words they were expected to say, sing or listen to, when their education and background in Christian faith was almost nil? "Blessed be the Lord God of Israel, for He hath visited and redeemed His people" . . . how do you relate words like these to the day-to-day experience of a shipyard apprentice?

To provide leisure-time facilities, and to make an opportunity for "organized friendship" with leaders of the club, was an excellent service for the church to perform – and the "octopus theory" was right to this extent, that if those facilities and opportunities had not been provided, it is difficult to see how the church could have been in touch at all with that section of the community. But had we ever thought through, I wondered, the rationale of our endeavours? To insist at all on church attendance seemed to me to vitiate the great gift we were offering: were we not thinking more of the welfare of the Church as an institution – that it should flourish numerically – rather than of the welfare of the boys? It struck me that the Church has always been tempted to care for numbers rather than for quality, and makes the mistake of equating a large congregation with a good congregation. Once that mistake is made (and of course, it is desperately easy to make it with the best of intentions, for obviously a large congregation is "a good thing"), it is very difficult to prevent manipulation, however subtle, from creeping in. I had begun to fear that what mattered most in the official eyes of the Church was not so much the sincerity of your attention, the quality of your worship, or even the depth of your commitment to the faith, but that you were there in your pew on a Sunday, and certainly in time to give your collection.

What I thought I saw in the gospels was the way in which Jesus always left the people He met free to accept or reject Him, and that what He had to offer was the very reverse of bribery: blood, toil, tears and sweat in the service of the Kingdom of God. I saw, in other words, that truly to be Christian our care for those boys had to be unconditional, and as I reflected on it, I saw that there was a deeper theological reason for this stress on being unconditional.

The starting point for all Christian faith is God's unconditional love for every one of us, since in Jesus Christ that love will ultimately triumph over every obstacle and opposition, not by force or manipulation, but simply by the power of its own attractiveness, its own persuasiveness. And that, in practice, means that we simply need to demonstrate that love: we do not need to try to manufacture a response, or feel constrained "to make things happen". (Later experience has confirmed me in this view: that the more we can put away all pretence at having influence, the more influence we have. That is an urgent paradox for Christians to learn.) We demonstrate: but the effect of our demonstration in the lives of others is entirely a matter for their own completely free response. That, incidentally, should absolve us of any sense of guilt if the institution doesn't flourish. The loving demonstration, the caring till it hurts, is in our hands: the response is not. And faith tells us that in the end (and, despite the confidence of so many sects in Christian history that they know when "the end" is, we are not given such knowledge), the victory of Love is assured.

It is strange how such an experience of a downtown boys' club led me to form such a theological view. But I was grateful for the lesson I learnt then in the early days of my ministry, for it sharpened the focus of my belief in pastoral care, and set it in a proper context. Of course, the battle wasn't over, and the pressure to serve the Church as an institution rather than be concerned about persons persisted.

After a second curacy in Barnard Castle, where I had the good fortune to work with Alan Webster, later to become Dean of St Paul's, I became Rector of Stretford Parish Church, a parish of thirteen thousand people, four miles from Manchester, certainly one of the happiest and busiest periods of my life. The pressure, as I say, continued. Each year, the Statistical Unit of the Church of England required a return about numbers of confirmation candidates, Christmas and Easter communicants and the like, the most significant figure in Church folk-lore being the number of Easter communicants. Were they down or up?

Further, my arrival at Stretford coincided with the advent of stewardship, whose aim, in practice, was to increase the Church's income, even if that aim was heavily over-larded by pretentious theological notions. Of course, we are all to be good stewards of God's bounty, and that means conscientious giving for the maintenance of the Church and for charitable objects. But the way in which stewardship worked

out in a parish was, it seemed to me, a denial of all
that is meant by the demonstration of God's unconditional love, the outpouring of His grace, a gift
given to us which we have done nothing to earn or
deserve. Good lay people were encouraged to knock
on the doors of parishioners who might not have
been visited by the church or in whom the church
might have shown not a scrap of interest over many
years, to ask them to pledge some money per week
for the upkeep of the church. ("After all, you'll need
the church when your daughter wants to be married
or your father buried – and you'll expect it to be well
maintained and warm!") The way stewardship was
presented and practised seemed to me to turn on
its head our notion of that grace which lies at the
heart of Christian faith. As I saw it, people would
only commit from their pockets once they became
committed as people, once they started to make a
response to a demonstration of love they had first
experienced. To ask for money first was again to use
people, and in any way to make people objects rather
than to treat them as subjects is to pervert Christian
faith.

Here then was another pointer in the direction of
unconditional pastoral care. It was strengthened still
further by my experience of parish visiting. It has
been one of the sadnesses in my later life to discover
what a low priority is given by clergymen today to the
importance of visiting in the parish beyond the more
immediate circumstances, where people are sick, in
trouble or bereaved. I know that there are a thousand
reasons for not visiting: that it is time-consuming,
that it can simply be a formal, polite exchange with
social boundaries so neatly defined as to exclude any

real meeting, that the pressures of administration and organization today are far greater than they were, and so on. Clearly in some circumstances, like those of inner city parishes, I grant that systematic visiting may well be almost impossible. But without subscribing to the old adage that "a house-going parson makes a church-going people" (and notice the impure motivation that seems to suggest!), it surely remains true that if the church as a loving community is going to show any care for those who live in the parish, but are not of it, visiting is essential. It represents a true act of grace, since it is to be done unconditionally, without expecting any obvious response, but simply out of love and concern.

My own particular pleasure as a parish priest was to visit those with whom the church had some slight contact – perhaps through a baptism a year or two ago, or the recent marriage of a son or daughter. The only thing which saddened me about the visits was the way in which my motivations were so often misinterpreted. Usually, I would not mention anything about the church, but try to keep the conversation focused on them, the family and so on. But soon, one of two things (or both!) would happen: they would start to give me extensive reasons why they couldn't be in church on a Sunday, or they would feel bold enough to say, "What have you *really* come for, Rector?" I thought how tragically pathetic it was that they could think that the only reason why the church was showing any interest in the household at all was so that it could get something out of it in the form of some return, churchgoing or financial.

Gradually, I found that as the years went by (and I had eleven years as Rector), the initial pressure I felt that the church should "do well" was lessening, and I was able, with local lay people, to relax and simply look for ways in which we could serve the needs of those in the parish. I have described elsewhere[1] one way in which we did this – through our street-warden scheme, linked to a group of people who were available to help in any emergency – but we were also able, for instance, to run an open lads' club every night of the week for any lad in the parish, and to provide a meeting place for the mentally handicapped once a week. I cannot adequately describe the sense of liberation which lay people feel when they are released from self-conscious "working for the church", which in practice often means persuading other people to give money to the church, or "trying to do something with" other people like "getting them to come", or making them be the recipients of words of "witness", which if they are not uttered, make good lay people feel guilty. Now I can almost hear the vociferous protests some people will make when they read these words, especially those who work hardest "to keep the church going", as they say. My point is that we are over-influenced by years of conventional thinking about the upkeep of the church, and I would argue that in the last analysis even the very survival of the church (as we know it) should not be a cause of great anxiety. In whatever form it is clothed, the loving community will always exist, and usually what we are fighting to preserve is not so much the essence but the trappings. It was said of the early Church, you remember, that it turned the ancient world upside down, and that at a time when its possessions and buildings were almost nil.

Let me illustrate what I mean from a recent

news item: that one out of every four churches in the country is stolen from, vandalized or set on fire every year. The obvious response to this phenomenon is to make objects in the church more secure, to increase insurance premiums, and above all to keep churches locked. In other words, a policy of simply hanging on to what you have got, at all costs. But there is another, and I would claim, supernatural, response, which is to keep as little as possible that is precious in the eyes of the world, and to give away the rest. We might then learn afresh of the simplicity of the Gospel, and the world might begin to see that we mean what we say when we *talk* about giving ourselves away, for the love of the world. What it sees at the moment, and these two news items came together, is that the Church Commissioners have increased their profits during the last year by 15 per cent. I have reason to be grateful personally for this increase, as it will mean an increase in my own pension. But what does this chasing after security and increased income say to the world about what we think is really important?

I have always thought that the best things which happen in church life are those which are totally unworthy of news coverage – and indeed, would be deformed if they were exposed to public gaze. Looking back now on my own experience of ministry, it isn't in any case the big things which remain vividly etched on my memory: the crowded harvest festivals, the large Easter communions and the like. Rather, it is *people*. The lady from Scotland, befriended by parishioners as she searched for her errant husband, the ex-prisoner from Strangeways

40

for whom we found some furnished living accommodation to give him a new start, and all seemingly to no avail; the mentally distraught lady who was helped to find a new life simply by the friendship of one or two parishioners. No noise: no fussy good-works busyness or self-importance about it, and certainly no self-conscious religious motivation; just a quiet Christian and human response to need, a true mark of pastoral care.

As I write this, it is twenty-two years since I left parish ministry as such. Only three years ago I was invited to a gathering of thirteen men and women, all of whom had been members of a group in the parish who had made themselves available in case of need. Only two still lived there; the rest were scattered as far afield as Scotland and Devon. One member had died, one had emigrated to the West Indies, one was looking after her desperately sick husband. Otherwise, all of them came to renew friendships and to bring the others up to date with their news. All of them, without exception, looked back on their time in the parish not merely as a happy time but as a seminal time, a true learning experience about the nature and purpose of the Church, an experience which had led them to take similar initiatives in the various places to which they had gone. And all, I believe, because they had seen something very simple: the priority of unconditional caring in the life of the Church, a "being available" for other people – and that had brought about a gaiety of spirit in them which was unmistakable.

CHAPTER FIVE

Chalk and Talk

In my fight in 1966 to remain a parish priest, against the wishes of the Bishop of the Diocese who had other ideas, I had to admit defeat. I was, to use his expression, "winkled out" to become a residentiary Canon of the Cathedral, and have responsibility for adult education in the Diocese. This responsibility was linked with becoming an honorary extra-mural staff tutor in Religious Studies in the University of Manchester.

The experience of being "winkled out" and leaving the parish taught me a great lesson in the mutuality of caring. As Rector of a large parish, there are many factors pushing you in the direction of self-importance, however much you recognize mentally that the graveyard is full of indispensables, and however highly you rate the theological status of the laity. You do rather come to think that it all, or at least nearly all, depends on you. Secretly, I suppose, I began to wonder how the parish would get on without me. The answer, of course, was that they would get on fine without me: the only person who suffered a bereavement was me! In my imagination, I was the one who was responsible for the caring; in effect, I was the one who was being cared for! It is this recognition of the mutuality of caring which keeps carers humble, and staves off all possibility of pretentiousness and pomposity.

I was to learn something else about caring, too, from my new responsibility in adult education: that there is no divergence between the pastoral role of the Church and its educational role; indeed, you cannot exercise the one without the other. I have already pointed to the example of a history master who inspired me to work hard in the Sixth Form, and that inspiration was a result of his care and his ability to see in me some sort of potential that I had never recognized in myself. My adult educational work confirmed that experience for me. I was engaged in organizing and teaching religious studies courses both in the University and in the region, and my teaching was related to my own discipline of pastoral theology. Courses are usually ten to twenty meetings, and the number of people who were prepared to sacrifice money and leisure time (sometimes in a three-year certificate course) in order to understand religious truth better, was most impressive.

I soon began to notice something else. As the course proceeded two things happened: first, and understandably, the group experience and group loyalty deepened and strengthened. That in itself can be a danger signal, in that as soon as students feel they have gained so much from and been enriched by that group experience, they are reluctant to see the group break up, and will try to devise all sorts of stratagems in order to perpetuate it. But groups must break up, lest the group which initially has enjoyed a learning and growth experience becomes a cosy and complacent closed circle. The second thing that happened was the increasing opportunities the course provided for members to ask honest questions about themselves, their own priorities and values, the direction their lives were taking, and so on. Being challenged intellectually about the roots and meaning of your faith means also that you are constantly being challenged as a whole person, since faith is as much to do with experience of life as it is with any intellectual understanding of Christian doctrine. So, as the course proceeded, students were increasingly ready to ask for counselling, not necessarily about some specific difficulty, but about the whole business of the relation between the changing nature of their faith and their own experience. Caring and teaching, thus, were working hand in hand – and that was excellent.

One factor which emerged troubled me greatly. Many of the students who enrolled in such Religious Studies courses were looking for something richer and at greater depth than their local church was able to give them, and came with a half-formed expectation and belief that they needed greater stimulus if they were to grow as they were meant to. They wanted, that is, to break out of the conformist and conventional role into which they felt they had been placed in church, in order better to discover themselves. It was because they found a greater degree of honesty and openness in the adult educational experience that they wanted to continue with the group, and that same honesty and openness made them increasingly dissatisfied with what they were experiencing in their local church Sunday by Sunday and week by week. What I longed to see happen was that they should take back into church life the vision they had caught and be "centres of dissatisfaction", catalysts of growth in that situation. Here was another sidelight on pastoral care: to nurture not those who are increasingly and complacently reconciled to situations, but those who are struggling rebelliously to alter those situations.

One of the most worthwhile and exciting adult educational exercises in which I have been regularly engaged for some years is helping lay people themselves to exercise more effective pastoral care. There are a lot of untapped resources and goodwill within our churches, and many more insights into caring available as a result of constant research that has gone on these last twenty or thirty years into subjects such as dying, bereavement, relationships, depression and so on. I felt that an important task was to marry these two, the goodwill and the insights, so that lay people could love and care with their heads as well as with their hearts.

Slowly, the idea of using these untapped resources to help in the overall pastoral task of the Church is growing, and certainly, more Anglican Dioceses are appointing bodies of "pastoral assistants", as they are called, all the time. (How some of them are used, how much responsibility they are given, and how far they are seen as doing jobs that the Vicar doesn't want to do, is another matter!) Many lay people are able to take on limited counselling roles, and it is possible – providing the limitations are strictly observed and after several weeks in an informal counselling course – for them to be of great help to those whom they know and meet who are suffering some emotional distress. We are not about the business of training amateur psychologists or psychiatrists. In trying to bring the considerable resources for helping within the community to bear upon the equally considerable human problems which beset that community, we cannot simply depend on the caring professions. We need to encourage all sorts of people to use resources for themselves as human beings, since most human needs can be and have always been met by those who aren't professionals. In any case, it is the quality of the human being, rather than any learned techniques, which in the end matters most in caring and counselling.

So, in our courses, our purpose is to lead to a greater understanding of human beings, how we relate to each other, how we can sustain each other at times of stress, marital conflict, depression and illness of all sorts. This often leads to greater sensitivity of faith, since now that faith will be seen in the context of real and pressing human needs.

The word "pastoral" has an unfortunate ring of "protectiveness" about it, as if it is the job of the pastor to protect his flock from being exposed to the sharp breezes of questioning and doubt, lest their faith freeze in the process. Angry reactions to the publication of books like *Honest to God* and *The Myth of God Incarnate*, and to the pronouncements of theologians like David Jenkins, well illustrate what I mean. They all show a deep insecurity, which is unworthy of a Christian attitude to truth.

I recall the way in which some years ago a group of three parishes joined together for Lent to pursue with me a simple course on Christian belief, in which we raised some of the difficulties ordinary people find with questions like the Virgin Birth and the Resurrection. I was interested to meet the Vicar

of one of the parishes after the course had finished.
"Don't worry," he said, "I'm getting them back to
the true faith . . ." We have so extolled the virtues of
simple, unquestioning faith, so fearfully encouraged
lay people in a passive obedient role that we do not
only make any questioning synonymous with disloy-
alty, but we often fail to bring out into the open as
we should the tension that is felt between what is
affirmed on Sundays and what is experienced on
week days.

My conviction, I repeat, is that the aim of the
adult educator and that of the pastoral carer are very
close: they are to foster the true independence, and
not dependence, of the person, his or her growing
maturity. Too often, both the processes of education
and caring are looked upon as there to create passive
belief, faith-receptacles and care-recipients. And the
subtle pressures upon both educators and carers to
exercise the pleasures of power over their charges
are manifold.

The words of the moral philosopher R. M. Hare,
about the dangers of indoctrination in education,
apply with equal force in the realm of caring, in
that both are subject to the great danger of creating
dependence and passivity.

> The educator is trying to turn children into
> adults: the indoctrinator is trying to make
> them into perpetual children. The educator
> is willing and hoping all the time for those
> whom he is educating to start thinking; and
> none of the thoughts that may occur to them
> are labelled "dangerous" a priori. The indoc-
> trinator, on the other hand, is watching for

signs of trouble, and ready to intervene
to suppress it when it appears, however
oblique and smooth his methods may be.
The difference between these two is like
the difference between the colonial admin-
istrator who knows, and is pleased, that he
is working himself out of a job, and the one
who is determined that the job shall still be
there even when he himself retires.

So there is, in the end, a very great
difference between the two methods. At the
end of it all, the educator will insensibly stop
being an educator, and find that he is talking
to an equal, to an educated man like himself
– a man who may disagree with everything he
has ever said; and unlike the indoctrinator,
he will be pleased. So, when this happens,
you can tell from the expression on his face
which he is.[1]

How far can we in the Church dare to be educators
rather than subtle indoctrinators?

CHAPTER SIX

A New Challenge

It was shortly after I had started my adult educational work that another and quite different challenge presented itself. Up to 1968, that is, for the first thirteen years during which commercial television had been in existence, the North West had been served by two different companies: for the first five weekdays by Granada Television, and for the weekend by ABC Television. In that year, ABC lost the franchise and Granada Television took on their weekend contractual obligations. This meant a corresponding change in their programme scheduling, for now Sundays would have to be included – and that, in turn, meant religion! Suddenly, Granada found itself with the task of appointing three religious advisers, which had become established practice for each television company, even though the sort of task on which they would be engaged and the sort of advice they would be expected to offer were very imprecise. What a prospect for a secular television company! Three black-coated clergymen, probably not even agreeing with each other, and certainly all of them coming from a world of communication eternally and infinitely removed from the instant world of the television screen, where even religion had to entertain as well as inform and educate . . .

No one was more surprised than I, then, to receive a telephone call at the Cathedral from the Education Officer at Granada (now to take over the role of Religious Programmes Officer as well), suggesting that we meet at the Kardomah Cafe, halfway between the two institutions, since there was something she wanted to discuss with me. It was to invite me to take up the position of Anglican Religious Adviser.

I have to confess that up to that moment my interest in and concern for religious television had been minimal, and frankly, so far as commercial television went, I had been over-influenced by the bilious attacks of Bernard Levin on the tawdriness and vulgarity of its programmes in the early days. I considered myself to be a staunch supporter of the BBC, and even a devoted follower of Lord Reith. So far as experience went, I had taken a hand in the preparations for the transmission of a Harvest Festival service from Barnard Castle fifteen years earlier, and I had preached twice on Radio Four and on the World Service. That was the sum total of my experience of the mass media. Whilst ABC was still in existence in the nineteen-seventies I was called for a "test" to see whether I were the right person to put over one or two Epilogues, or "Spiritual Horlicks", as they are known in the trade. But since I was never called again, I obviously failed the test. And that wasn't a very promising start for a would-be practitioner! I marvel now at my audacity in accepting an advisory role at all.

Nor was my confidence increased on the very first occasion I set foot inside the building, clad in a dog-collar on a Friday afternoon in November 1968.

I had it reported to me that someone, as soon as soon as he saw my collar, he shouted. "A bloody parson! We don't want bloody parsons in here!" Perhaps he was only echoing what sober people in the company were thinking, but were too polite to say.

But it was clear that our role as advisers was ambivalent. We were, for instance, appointed by the company and not by the Church, a fact which has often been misunderstood within the Church itself: we are not church delegates, nor even spokesmen for the Church, but just ourselves. That could, in difficult circumstances, create a divided loyalty, although I have to say after twenty years' experience, that there has been more misunderstanding on the Church's part than on that of the company. Then again, in the role itself, advice can only be given when asked for and may be rejected. That was a lesson in humility important to learn. Too often ministers believe that their professional knowledge of the Gospel enables them to dictate how the Gospel should be communicated. But in general we in the Church, over the past five hundred years, have lost the art of visual communication, even though in the parables of Jesus, the original form was visual. We have come to think that because we are professionals, theoretically speaking, we can therefore be imaginative and creative in our use of this new art form and devise good religious television.

What slowly dawned on us was that only a partnership could possibly produce happy results, and that in turn meant not only an open and trusting relationship between the three of us as Advisers –

Dr Arthur Chadwick, Father Vincent Whelan and myself – but also with our Producer, Peter Heinze, and anyone else in the company with whom we were to work. In every respect we have been fortunate. For twenty years there has only been one break in "the team" and that was when, eighteen months ago, our Catholic Adviser and friend died suddenly, and was replaced by an equally acceptable colleague, Father Michael Child. Peter Heinze, the Producer with whom we have worked, isn't a committed Christian and would find the description "honest searcher" the most appropriate that could be applied to him. Occasionally, when I have had cause to mention this in church circles, there has been a gasp of horror. How could an agnostic possibly produce good religious programmes? I stress again that it has been a partnership. And in the course of my time in Granada, it has been a salutary experience to have been asked more difficult questions about the Christian faith and its implications, and more especially, about the "cash value" in human terms of the theological statements we so much take for granted in church.

There was another important lesson to learn. Religious people outside the television world often complain that those of us inside are not "getting the message across", as if we are timid of the message or not shouting loudly enough! As if, for instance, the medium of television was just another form of the verbal or literary medium. But television is an art form in its own right, and demands its own respect. Very often, in talking with church groups, I have discovered that they see only the vast opportunities television presents – usually, I have to say, for propaganda! – without seeing any of its limitations, or the way in which it is always a reductionist exercise. The excellent innovative idea for a programme may not come to fruition at all, because it can't be "translated" into the visual. For instance, if the subject is a historical subject, it is quite possible that the relevant visuals simply do not exist. I recall that when we were making "The Christians" series, which Bamber Gascoigne presented, and wished to illustrate the burgeoning of Protestant revolt before the Reformation, we had to concentrate more on John Hus of Bohemia than on John Wycliffe of Lutterworth in this country, not necessarily because he was more significant in any assessment of major influences, but simply because the pictures were better! That is to say, there was hardly anything actually to show of the events of Wycliffe's life or the history of Lollardry.

Kenneth Clark, in his television series "Civilization",[1] made something of the same point when he talked about what through the limitations of television he was forced to leave out of account. He found himself in difficulty, he said, with regard to law and philosophy, because he couldn't think of any way to make them "visually interesting". Since, like law and philosophy, religion is concerned with the development, clarification and propagation of ideas, it suffers from the same difficulty. That is why, of course, so much religious television has featured "talking heads", in discussions which were probably more suitable to radio than television. (Irrelevant details like the pattern on a man's tie can often distract viewers from following an argument closely on television.)

Characteristically, our first experiment in general religious programming in 1969-70 was cerebral rather than visual in nature. Called "Seven Days", a title used recently by Yorkshire Television for a programme with some similarities (does Yorkshire steal all its ideas from across the Pennines?), it attempted to explore moral and ethical issues behind some of the major events of each week. In addition to the studio audience, chosen to represent different points of view, there were two or three "experts" and always one person to voice what Christian faith would have to say about the issue. This was usually the future Bishop of Birmingham, Hugh Montefiore. We lived somewhat on our nerves, in that we rarely knew until Thursday what topic we would be dealing with in the recording on Friday, so the themes and persons to be involved had to be summoned up quite hastily. Further, we ran into difficulties as to whether the programmes were sufficiently "religious".

There are many differing criteria that can be applied in order to decide this question, but one of those criteria that we have never allowed to influence us at Granada is what might be called the "formal" religious content, that is, ecclesiastical themes and churchy subjects. We have always maintained, and have on occasions argued with the Independent Broadcasting Authority (IBA) in this respect, that it is the point at which faith has a cutting edge in the world and in the lives of ordinary people which should be our main concern. With "Seven Days", it had its cutting edge in social, political and economic affairs, but the stance we took in this first religious series of ours presaged that which was to influence us much later in our series of Air Care Meditations.

It surfaced again in another series, "Private Lives", in which the well-known film maker Denis Mitchell explored the private lives of seven different characters, to discover, as they say, "what made them tick", and how faith or lack of faith influenced them. It was a remarkable feat on Denis Mitchell's part to have penetrated so far into the real hearts of those he was exploring (without being seen himself) – but there again we were criticized by an Evangelical in a letter to *The Times* for not being "religious enough", heedless of the fact that if the Gospel they and we were so keen to proclaim were to be seen to have any credibility, it could only have that credibility if it were reaching the depths of people's lives.

In our transmission of church services, we have always tried to reflect different traditions in the three branches of the Church we represent, and to strike a balance between different sorts of churchmanship and the geographical area in which the church stands. So on one Sunday, we might transmit Matins according to the 1662 Book of Common Prayer, from a small church in the country, and in our next transmission, Parish Communion, using the alternative Services Book, from a large church in an inner city parish. Our allocation is roughly six services a year: three Anglican, two Free Church, one Roman Catholic. In the early days, our choice of church was dictated by which football match we were recording, so that the outside-broadcast crews didn't have too far to travel – another lesson in humility for us! – but in later years our choice has been largely determined by variety and balance. Of course, it helps to have a choir which can sing in tune, and clergymen who can take a service well and preach an inspiring sermon, but we don't regard ourselves as being there to put on a show. We simply wish to reflect as faithfully as possible the worship of that particular church on that particular Sunday. To that end, we alter the service as little as possible and ask the congregation to forget the TV equipment they see around them, and worship as they would on an "ordinary Sunday". For we believe that if they do, the sincerity and reality of their worship will communicate to those watching at home. The majority of viewers of church services are the elderly and the sick, that is, those who used to go to church, but who now for some physical reason are prevented from doing so, and they number somewhere between a half and three-quarters of a million people.

Over the years (and we have now been responsible for something like a hundred and twenty church services) we have quite naturally had our trials and frustrations, as well as our humorous and happy occasions. For instance, the Vicar of the country parish who suddenly in the midst of a sermon produced a letter from an Indian boy who needed money for his training as a priest, and asked the viewers for donations! "He's had £35,000 worth of advertising time", said our Director . . . The minister who ten minutes before we went on air threatened to take away the bread and wine he'd brought for the communion service unless he were given a greater part in the service . . . The Vicar who got so carried away by his own oratory that he preached ten minutes longer than he should have done . . . But by taking and transmitting the original church service, and refusing to dress it up, we are reflecting church life as it is, warts and all.

CHAPTER SEVEN

A Failed Experiment

As time went on, we began to ask ourselves whether, in the transmission of church services, we were making the best use of the hour allotted to us for religious purposes. True, we were serving the interests of an important minority in linking them to a live church service, helping them to worship through it, and keeping alive for them old associations. But was there something else we could do which could still be a personal help to that small minority, and yet appeal to a larger and more representative section of the community? We were not impressed by attempts made by other companies at devised services from the studio, which seemed to have about them an air of artificiality. Could we not, perhaps, devise a meditation, centring around a personal theme, which might include some of the elements of a church service, but which would attempt to speak more directly to the viewer? We saw that meditation not as replacing, but as supplementing, our outside broadcast church services.

So we made our first experiment, focused on the theme of "Joy", in June 1974, exploring its theological dimension and its relevance to human life, using biblical and secular readings, and music, both sacred and secular, played on the piano. It was not gripping. As we look back on it now, we can see how wooden it was, and how little it would speak to our viewers personally. But our failure did not deter us from believing that there were possibilities in the format which needed further exploration. So we tried again.

Three years later, in October 1977, we produced our second meditation on "Forgiveness", and in April 1978 our third on "Loneliness". We included in both these meditations a new element of an interview with people like Lady Ewart-Biggs, whose husband, a member of the Diplomatic Service, was killed by IRA terrorists. That element of interview brought a much greater sense of reality to the meditations, but we were still not very satisfied. Perhaps, we thought with great daring, we should try not just one meditation but a series. So we opted to do seven consecutive meditations on the Sundays in the season of Lent and on Easter Day. They were recorded in the studio. We took "Discipleship" as our theme, with Father Michael Hollings as the writer and presenter, and John Franklyn Robbins, the actor, as the reader.

The subjects of Discipleship we explored were: the call to us from Jesus; our sacrifice; what is demanded of us in answering that call; our temptation to take the wrong way on our journey; our failure when we give in to the temptations; our guilt when we realize and acknowledge our failure; our faith which guides us and helps us through our difficulties; and lastly, our hope of things to come, both here and now and in eternal life.

For the first time, interestingly, and without asking for any response, after our transmissions something like fifty viewers wrote with appreciative com-

ments; only one viewer strongly disliked the meditation, calling it "satanic and highly dangerous" – even
though we still don't know why! The television critic
of the Catholic journal *The Universe* said that it was
one of the most effective television aids to prayer he
had ever seen.

Still believing that we were on the right road
but without necessarily getting very far along it,
we devised another series for the following year, but
this time for the season of Advent and Christmas: a
series of six meditations on "The Gifts of God". The
subjects I presented were: our universe; our selves;
our achievements; our search for meaning in life; our
Lord; and lastly our Church.

The format and ingredients were largely the same,
but this time we recorded most of the meditations
in the Catholic Adviser's church of St Boniface,
Salford. Again, without asking for it, we had a
considerable number of letters from viewers who
simply wished to express their thanks for something
which, as one viewer said, "comforted, challenged
and encouraged in healthy proportion". Only one
viewer out of nearly eighty called it a "miserable
dirge".

In all these, our first faltering attempts at meditations, we were encouraged by the IBA's Religious
Programmes Officer, Christopher Martin, who said
that we had "chanced upon a winning way of using
the full resources of television to go across its natural
grain and make the people sit very still". Further,
he produced evidence that the meditations had "attracted and held not just churchgoers, or people who
would claim to be 'religious'. They did in fact hold
such viewers, but also won an audience of others,

giving them, sometimes for the first moment in their lives, a glimpse into the mysteries of God."

Clearly it was time for us to go further. Was there a better way still of relating television to the personal needs of some viewers?

In 1978 in Bath, at the Sixth Religious Consultation promoted by the IBA, Cardinal Hume had asked the question, "Should we attempt to build Christian work in radio and television into the total pastoral strategy of our churches? When the broadcast is over, and when men and women have perhaps been moved, is there anything that the local church can do?" Here the Archbishop was obviously feeling his way towards some sort of pastoral strategy as a follow-up service, which would involve the local church as well as the broadcasters. Our thoughts were tending in the same direction.

If, however, we were going to devise a workable system, we would have to look first at society and assess the sort of needs to which we would be responding, the most deeply felt but often little expressed human needs. The question we were asking was, can television have a role in this area of individual need? At first sight the question seemed absurd. Traditionally, men and women looked to religion to supply comfort and solace in times of distress, and further to give shape and meaning to their lives when all seems pointless. But the decline of the Church and the advent of the welfare state have meant that people have looked elsewhere for that comfort, and the pastoral role of the ministry is not as clear or self-evident as it was, for instance, in the days of Richard Baxter and George Herbert in the seventeenth century. Nevertheless religion was there, Sunday by Sunday, on our television screens, and whatever format the service takes, amongst the mixed bag of letters which come in afterwards (some from cranks, some asking for information about a hymn tune) there are always a few heart-rending letters (some anonymous, which makes them even more heart-rending) which cry out for action.

So we began to feel that if this is true of those televised services for which no particular response was sought, what might the response be if services of worship were deliberately framed which had individual needs in mind from the start and which provided a co-ordinated, quietly executed, pastoral back-up system? The answer, of course, was that we did not know, since we had no evidence from real experimentation to help us. The fast-growing electronic church across the Atlantic, with its staggering figures of viewer response to appeals for money, had little to tell us here. It was not primarily addressing itself to the individual needs we have described; but we have to admit that that church would not have succeeded at all unless it had touched a personal nerve and sensed the hunger of many people to be "in touch". That is true even when we reject the impersonal, computerized pastoral care which, at its best, it offers to viewers.

We had a sort of hunch that there is a mass of lonely, distressed people "out there" who do not know where to turn to in their misery and loneliness, who are not necessarily in touch with any organized church, who somehow believe that religion and things connected with religion have something to offer them. We started to think that under proper safeguards of confidentiality and a respect for their freedom to reject our offer, they might request help from a properly and discreetly organized pastoral support system, having, first of all, had their needs illuminated and explored through some sort of meditation, specially designed for this purpose.

It was fortunate that at the time that we were asking these questions and looking into the future, our Producer, Peter Heinze, was able, with the blessing and encouragement of Granada, and contracted by the IBA, to conduct a two-month period of research into the feasibility of such a television ministry. The report he produced was the fruit of many conversations and much wide-ranging thought, and his conclusion was that a modest experiment should be set up to test the water (air?), and that Granada should be the company to conduct it.

Of course, as the report made clear, the concept of a pastoral strategy linked to television and radio programmes wasn't original. We have all been familiar for some time with the phone-in programme linked to broadcasts, which invite the participation of the viewer and attempt to respond to requests for help. Westward Television (as it was then) for several years ran a special Epilogue four times a year, which asked viewers to respond to matters raised in the programme. After transmission eight telephones were manned for an hour and a half to answer calls, most of which were described as being of "a pastoral nature". On several occasions I had taken part as a telephone counsellor in Radio Manchester's "Late Night Line", chaired by Ralph Birtwistle, which counsels people on air, usually on specific subjects. I have to confess that sometimes

I felt unhappy about the role in which I was being fixed, and the expectations which were being fostered in the minds of the listeners. If you are designated as a counsellor, that implies "expert", and an "expert" implies the ability to give "advice". But I maintain that the only advice which it is legitimate for a counsellor to give is information – often about agencies, for instance, where further help can be obtained. I am mindful, too, of the warning issued by the psychiatrist Willard Gaylin, the President of the Hastings Centre, an American research institute devoted to ethical issues in the field of medicine and mental health: "The diagnoses are always glib, and it's got to be bad advice if all you have is a voice over the phone . . . these people are giving specific guidance after just a few minutes on the phone. It is hard enough to do that after an hour with a patient in the office."[1] All this we had to bear in mind in any pastoral support system we devised, to ensure that our counselling by phone was "listening and/or linking" – and not advice-giving.

We were aware, too, from the start of our experiment, of the danger of creating expectations in viewers which we could not fulfil: dangers that our counsellors would be seen to be "problem solvers", and a danger that we should not have the resources to be able to cope with the number of callers after each transmission. So we decided to proceed cautiously with our first experiment, since we felt that it would be better not to offer any help at all than to have to disappoint people in such a personal and delicate area. Accordingly, although the programmes were networked, help was only offered after their transmission in the Granada region, and our initial approach to viewers was extremely low key: a station announcer's voice over a caption at the end of the service. In retrospect, we can see clearly that our approach was far too cautious and the response was negligible. But we made serious miscalculations, too, in the programmes themselves. We had decided to adopt one of the suggestions made to Peter Heinze in the "Air Care" report: "The first half hour could examine a theme, say Forgiveness, in the way any television programme might examine anything, with the normal resources that a television company has. The actual worship in the second part would incorporate the theme into its part of the programme. In this way, the non-committed viewer might be attracted at least to the first part."

So we chose six churches in the region (three Anglican, two Free Church, one Roman Catholic) from which to conduct our experiment in May and June 1983, and proceeded on those lines of taking the theme of the service from the Bible reading for the day. But we made the mistake of using existing church groups to stimulate exploration of those themes by means of discussion. Now whilst we might quite rightly have hoped that the viewer would identify with the "ordinary person" who was honestly expressing his difficulties in the discussion, our hopes of coherent discussion were largely frustrated, and must have left viewers confused about the theme. It wasn't the fault of the "ordinary people"; they struggled hard and well, but we were asking too much of them, and certainly of the local parson who, whatever his virtues, isn't necessarily the best person to elicit insights and facilitate discussions. Further, we were probably unwise to use outside broadcast services of worship at all for the particular purpose we had in mind. In their inevitable use of weighty theological affirmations and heavy liturgical language, they seemed to distance Christian faith and the Church just at the point where we hoped they would be seen to be real and relevant, and as resources to those in trouble. In addition, the themes arising out of the Bible readings were sometimes too vague and diffuse (e.g. "community", "freedom") to relate directly to viewers' most personal difficulties. We had to think again.

CHAPTER EIGHT

Our Jolly List

In July/August 1985, we transmitted three specially devised Acts of Meditation, and have roughly followed the same pattern in subsequent transmissions. The ingredients are:

1 Exploration of the theme, both in its psychological and religious dimensions.
2 Biblical and secular readings related to that theme.
3 Interviews with those who are undergoing, or have undergone, difficulties to which the theme is pointing.
4 Hymns and poetry.
5 Music and organ solos.
6 Film and photographic stills to illustrate aspects of the theme.
7 Prayers and silence.

We recognized from the start that the use of the word "Meditation" might create ambiguity in some people's minds. Usually, of course, it denotes a religious discipline or exercise, common to many religions, designed to nourish faith and spiritual growth. Sometimes meditation focuses on specific religious subjects, like God the Holy Spirit. Strictly speaking, we intended to do neither of these things, whilst incorporating elements of both of them! That is to say, our intention was to nourish faith and growth, and to concentrate on one subject a programme, but we were determined not to end up with theological abstractions and niceties. So we deliberately chose themes which would reflect viewers' real experiences of life and in particular, perhaps, the more sombre aspects of that experience with which we all have to struggle. However, within each of these themes there isn't only a psychological aspect, but also a religious or faith element, and it was the combination of these two which gave a distinctive flavour to the meditations.

Similarly, whilst there have often been phone-ins provided on the topics we covered (especially, for instance, on handicap, dying and bereavement), our specific intention was to involve faith as an integral part of the programme, not in order to give facile answers or minimize the difficulties, but to illuminate these difficulties and thus do greater justice to the wholeness of the person involved.

One aspect of traditional meditation we were determined not to lose, and that was its reflective nature. Television orthodoxy often deems that programmes are "pacy" (to use the jargon), with the implication that shots must change quickly and speakers not be given longer than a minute or two to make their point. Contrary to this, we were deliberately slow and lingering, allowing viewers time and space to quieten any restlessness, and to concentrate on that which was being seen and heard. Hence the use of the word Meditation. We did not want to use the words "service of worship" to describe our meditations, since although they contained elements to be found in any such service, like hymns, lessons and prayers, they weren't liturgical services at all in the strict sense of the word, but rather, religious reflections on a theme. To reach more deeply and specifically into the theme than is possible with any general presentation, it was essential to have other authorities in the form of readings from relevant sources, both biblical and secular. Occasionally, where the language was accessible and not over-laden with jargon, we used readings from theological works.

Indispensable, in my view, were the interviews with people who were suffering or had suffered from the particular theme we were exploring. It is comparatively easy to talk about other people's troubles: it is much more difficult to be challenged by them in person! Without doubt, these interviews have given us some of the most moving moments of the meditations, as some of the examples I quote later will show. There was one besetting sin of Christian apologists we especially wished to avoid. Paul Tillich, the American theologian, used to say that Christians and the Church are excellent at answering questions no one is asking! I would add that they are often very good at providing neat and slick answers to difficult personal questions, without fully entering into the complexity of those questions. So we didn't wish to interview those who had been "successful at coping" with their difficulties, and for whom the problem was solved, with the implication that "if only you were like me" or "if only you had my faith", then your difficulties would dissolve too.

What we were looking for was people who were still perhaps struggling in the darkness, but able to see one or two rays of light, and who could point to resources they had discovered of which previously they had been quite unaware. Then, because they were "ordinary people", although perhaps somewhat extraordinary in the way in which they were handling their difficulties, those watching could be given hope, not through some "pious message" but through the real experiences of real people.

Music of course is essential, but what and how? We found this a more difficult question than we had imagined. Hymns present a special problem. It becomes all too easy in composing church services, to use hymns as "fillers", without too much regard to the words, on the spurious grounds that the congregation like singing hymns and really care much more about the tunes than they do about the words. (The truth of this statement can easily be decided by putting a familiar hymn to an unfamiliar tune.) But since it is almost certainly the case that popular theology is substantially derived more from singing hymns than from any direct teaching from the pulpit, a careful choice of the words of hymns becomes essential. For us, it wasn't only a matter of selecting words which illuminate the particular difficulty the programme was exploring: it was that of not suddenly appearing to escape into a religious world where difficulties instantly dissolve. So often the very lofty aspirations and exalted sentiments of hymns are in great contrast to the situation of the viewer, who is able to identify with the "downbeat" theme of the programme more than rise to the aspirations of the hymn. For instance, how many would wish for

> a thousand tongues
> to sing my great redeemer's praise . . .

or something like it?

So, just at the point where you are trying to focus on real life situations, the abstractions that hymns sometimes present take you somewhere else! Accordingly, in the meditations we have become much more mindful of C. S. Lewis's judgement that "we need fewer hymns and better hymns – and chiefly fewer!" We tended to choose relevant verses of hymns rather than the whole hymn itself, most of which are in any case much too long, especially when they are simply being listened to. We have never quite solved to our satisfaction the question as to whether we should use a robed choir or a simple quartet to sing the hymns. Some of us believe that choirs are better heard than seen – but what, then, do we show on the screen, for something like three or four minutes? Other music we used were solo organ pieces of a reflective character and music on disc, usually over stills.

Our use of silence in our times of prayer was quite a challenge, and we pride ourselves, I hope rightly, on being the first television station to pioneer its use. Since a prerequisite of television and radio seems to be that there must be continuous sound, we thought that people would be phoning to say that there was something wrong with their set, as they didn't seem to be getting any sound! But silence doesn't only cut across the grain of standard media practice: it also runs contrary to the tone and temper of the age. I would have to add that even in church these days, where we are often encouraged in the "family spirit" and where noise seems to be regarded as indicative of vitality, the ability to sustain silence is equally a sign of vitality, and certainly more enriching than continual noise. We wanted our viewers to have space in which to reflect on what was being said, and relate it to their own circumstances; and we often wanted them to intercede for other people without the necessity of a form of words. I have discovered that the older I get, the more simply I want to pray, and in praying for other people, have concluded that simply to name them in God's presence (which is another way of surrounding them with His love) is all that I want to do; name them, that is, in silence. During our silence in the meditations we focused on a simple cross as the visual image.

So what were the subjects for the meditation, and on what principle did we choose them? We thought it right to select those experiences which weigh most heavily upon us at different times in our lives. They often impinge more heavily upon us still when we do experience them, because of our genuine unwillingness to look at them, and the general "conspiracy of silence" which surrounds them. We often referred to the list of subjects jokingly as our "jolly list" or our "anti-ratings war" . . .

We began with an experience which affects us all at some time in our lives, the experience of bereavement, the process of which has been so well researched in the course of the past twenty years. There is a wealth of insight now available, thanks to the devoted labours of John Bowlby, Colin Murray Parkes and others, into what happens to those who

71

are bereaved – both in the way they are treated by other people and how they react to their experience. So it was part of our purpose to make those insights more available, and to help not only the bereaved themselves and those who were seeking to help the bereaved, but also to prepare all our viewers for the experience when it eventually touched them. I found that this was very much in line with what I had been seeking to do in my adult educational work in the pastoral care courses I had taught. Of course we were not the first to produce a programme on the subject of bereavement. Since society's taboos on the subject of death and bereavement have slowly been broken over the past few years, there have been a few television documentaries on the subject, and much writing from different perspectives. What we were seeking to do was to marry the insights research had given us with the insights which come from religious faith – and so open up the wholeness of the subject. At the same time, we wanted to speak personally to the viewer so that without patronizing or talking down to him or her, he or she could feel that we were alongside them if they had recently experienced bereavement.

We used two readings from Christian writers as far apart as the fifth and twentieth centuries; one by St John Chrysostom, writing to a widow about the death of her husband:

> I grant you that all the world over amongst men there have been few like your husband, so affectionate, so gentle, so humble, so sincere, so understanding, so devout. And certainly if he had altogether perished, and

utterly ceased to be, it would be right to be
distressed, and sorrowful; but if he has only
sailed into the tranquil haven, and taken his
journey to Him who is really his king, one
ought not to mourn but to rejoice on these
accounts. For this death is not death, but
only a kind of emigration and translation
from the worse to the better, from earth to
heaven, from men to angels, and Him who
is the Lord of angels and archangels.

Wherefore in proportion as you grieve
that God has taken away one who was so
good and worthy you ought to rejoice that he
has departed in much safety and honour and
is in great peace and tranquillity. For is it not
out of place to acknowledge that heaven is far
better than earth, and yet to mourn those
who are translated from this world to the
other? For if that blessed husband of thine
had been one of those who lived a shameful
life contrary to what God approved it would
have been right to bewail and lament for him
not only when he departed, but whilst he
was still living; but in as much as he was
one of those who are the friends of God we
should take pleasure in him not only whilst
living but also when he has been laid to
rest. But perhaps you long to hear your
husband's words, and enjoy the affection
which you bestowed on him, and you yearn
for his society, and the glory which you had
on his account, and the splendour, and honour and security, and all these things being
gone distress and darken your life. Well, the

affection which you bestowed on him you
can keep now just as you formerly did.

For such is the power of love, it embraces,
and unites, and fastens together not only
those who are present and near, and visible
but also those who are far distant; and neither length of time nor separation in space,
nor anything else of that kind can break up
and sunder in pieces the affection of the
soul.[1]

The twentieth-century piece was from a Catholic
author, Henri Nouwen, whose writings have become
very popular recently. It was a *Letter of Consolation*
written to his father after the death of his mother,
and it was encouraging that even though they were
so far apart in time, the two writers were expressing
the same truth.

Our quiet joyful waiting is much deeper
than wishful thinking. It is waiting with the
knowledge that love is stronger than death,
and that this truth will become visible to
us. How, When, Where? These questions
keep rushing into our impatient hearts. Yet
when we experience that quiet, joyful waiting, they cease troubling us and we feel that
all is well.[2]

It was, however, my interview with two ladies,
both of whom had recently suffered bereavements,
but of different sorts, that I found most illuminating
and moving – and from viewers' comments, I know
that that was true of them, too.

74

Alice, a Catholic whose husband had died of a coronary, told of an incident from her school days. She had been educated in a strict Catholic convent and found one of her teachers to be, as she described her, an absolute dragon. One day one of her friends was caught reading *Woman* magazine in the cloakroom, and all the class was put into detention, told what heathens they were and instructed to pray for the forgiveness of God. The culprit told the Sister that she found it very difficult to pray, and the Sister's reply was, "When you can't pray, that is the time when you should really try". Ironically, it was this thought that came to Alice's mind in the early stages of her bereavement, and it helped her a lot. She was able to turn to prayer and found it a great support. "Without prayer", she said, "my life doesn't function." She spoke sadly, but without bitterness, about the way in which some people avoided her "because they were afraid to become involved", just at the time when she needed most support. "If only they'd realize that perhaps just a word or even just a touch on the arm would mean so much, and even if the person cried, perhaps they needed them to cry and to be with someone who cried."

Helen had lost a daughter, Rachel, aged seven and a half, nine months previously and we were talking together in the churchyard only a few yards away from where Rachel was buried. Helen explained how empty and devastated she still felt, and how she (unlike Alice) had been quite unable to pray. However, she had found in friends a great support – but with a difference. Realizing how awkward people felt in the presence of someone who is bereaved, Helen said that in the early days she made a conscious effort herself to try either to speak to or meet friends as quickly as possible; and then to mention Rachel's name, and get over the initial awkwardness. So the bereaved Helen was the person ready to take initiatives! She said she had been on the other end of that experience and knew how one doesn't know what to say to anybody who has lost someone close to them. But she wanted Rachel talked about, because otherwise it would have been almost to deny that she ever existed. "I didn't want people to forget her that quickly", she said . . .

The churchyard I refer to in Helen's interview was that of Nether Alderley church in Cheshire, a medieval church in a country setting which was just right for our purpose. We used the choir of St Ann's, Manchester, under Ronald Frost, and for the readings the well-known actor and actress, Peter Barkworth and Cherie Lunghi. The first three meditations were transmitted in July and August 1985, and the second three in October 1985.

Let me now highlight some themes and features from our next five meditations.

Our second subject was that of Failure. I remarked how flattered I had once been when I was asked to speak to a group of people from my own personal experience of failure! The truth is, of course, that we are all, without exception, failures in some sense or another, and when we try to divide up the world into those who are "successful" and those who are "failures" what we are really describing is those who have been successful *at* something or have failed *at* something. The trouble starts when we fail at something – in a marriage, for instance, or in getting promotion at work, or even in getting any work at all, and we begin to feel that we are failures – and

that often means that we start going downhill fast.
I was trying to say that the only failure that really
matters in the end is the failure to be a certain sort
of person, and the only success that is worthwhile
is to be a certain sort of person. Oddly enough,
the person who has failed at many things may be
more of a success as a human being than the one
who appears to have everything in life. He or she
may well have used their failure to make themselves
stronger human beings and more mature. So, since
we all share a common humanity, and since each
one of us is made in God's image, God's unique
and loved creature, the words "success" and "failure" aren't words we can properly apply to human
beings. And once we begin to see that we are here
on this earth not to achieve success, but to be fully
human beings, then we needn't pretend any more.
There is a great deal of pressure on us these days
to pretend to be the success we know in our heart
of hearts that we aren't – or to make compensation
for our failure.

To look at Jesus is illuminating in this respect.
He was a model human being, and has remained so
for millions of people through many generations. But
He went to His death as an abject failure in the eyes
of the world. He had done many good deeds, healed
many sick people, fed the hungry multitude – but
where were they all when He was crucified? He had
taught crowds of people about the love of God – and
when He needed most support, where were they? He
made disciples who shared many of His experiences –
and when the going got rough, they all "forsook Him
and fled". For three years' ministry, and service to all
who needed Him, He had hardly anything to show.

In other words, He was hardly "successful" as success is commonly understood today – and yet as a model human being, He was one of the most successful of all. And of course, after the Resurrection the disciples on reflection glimpsed the truth of this.

In the programme, I spoke with George, who had been unemployed and was now himself helping unemployed young people. George and his wife had been in full lay service in the Salvation Army, as managers of a hostel and a canteen. They were dedicated people, believing themselves to be just where God wanted them to be. "I couldn't envisage doing anything other than just what I was doing: my future was mapped out" – or so he thought. Soon, however, tensions began to develop in their marriage, and it was suggested to them by the Salvation Army that they should withdraw from their officership, which they did. George felt not only that he had failed in his job, but that he had failed Christ, and was now no use to anybody. He lost more and more self-confidence, so much so that in the space of two years he had moved from being a Salvation Army officer to the status of being a dosser in a Salvation Army hostel. It was a complete reversal of roles. But as with so many others, a sense of failure led to a reappraisal of his life. He began, he said, to find a faith that was deeper and wider than that which he'd previously experienced, and he and his wife tentatively started to rebuild their relationship – on a much more honest basis. Consequently, his self-confidence started to return and he began to work for an organization which helps unemployed youth, those who too feel themselves to be failures. (I learnt recently that since that interview George has successfully completed a university degree course.)

George's talk of the unemployed made me realize how this division we make between those who are "successful" and those who are "failures" makes the lot of the unemployed much worse. Ever since we became an industrial nation, we have tended to see men and women as valuable only in so far as they keep the wheels of industry and commerce turning. So a person becomes important, not in himself and for himself, but only in so far as he makes a practical contribution to the successful running of those wheels. We come very close to thinking of all those who aren't able to contribute (often through no fault of their own) as shirkers or scroungers. But it isn't our practical contribution that matters; it is what we are in ourselves, especially when we know in our heart of hearts that we are precious as people.

An anonymous poem from the fourteenth century speaks well of this preciousness, of the way in which God's love rests in each of us, whatever our failure.

> But art Thou come, dear Saviour? hath Thy love
> Thus made Thee stoop, and leave Thy throne
>   above,
> Thy lofty heavens, and thus Thyself to dress
> In dust to visit mortals? Could no less
> A condescension serve? And after all
> The mean reception of a crib and stall?
> Dear Lord, I'll fetch Thee thence! I have a
>   room
> ('Tis poor, but 'tis my best) if Thou wilt come
> Within so small a cell, where I would fain
> Mine and the world's Redeemer entertain.

I mean, my heart: 'tis sluttish, I confess,
And will not mend Thy lodging, Lord, unless

Thou send before Thy harbinger, I mean
Thy pure and purging Grace, to make it clean

And sweep its nasty corners; then I'll try
to wash it also with a weeping eye

And when 'tis swept and wash'd, I then will go
And, with Thy leave, I'll fetch some flowers
    that grow

In Thine own garden, Faith and Love, to Thee;
With these I'll dress it up, and these shall be

My rosemary and bays. Yet when my best
Is done, the room's not fit for such a guest.

But here's the cure; Thy presence, Lord, alone
Will make a stall a court, a crib a throne.

A hymn of William Blake, "The Divine Image",
summed up what we had been trying to say in this
meditation about the way in which, irrespective of
what we have or have not got, of what we can or
cannot do, of our success or failure at achieving
things, we are all valuable to God and therefore
worthy of respect from other people.

To Mercy, Pity, Peace and Love
All pray in their distress;
And to these virtues of delight
Return their thankfulness.

For Mercy, Pity, Peace and Love
Is God our Father dear;
And Mercy, Pity, Peace and Love
Is man, His child and care.

For Mercy has a human heart,
Pity, a human face,
And Love, the human form divine,
And Peace, the human dress.

Then every man, of every clime,
That prays in his distress,
Prays to the human form divine,
Love, Mercy, Pity, Peace.

Our next exploration, the following week, was of
the feeling of Pointlessness in life. Probably when
we ask the question "What's the point?" we are
not really expecting an answer: we are protesting
against the coldness and deadness we feel inside,
the way in which life doesn't seem to add up any
more. It's as though life has lost its heart, as though
it's difficult to find any real purpose and meaning.
In the programme, I tried to make a response to
the question, "What's the point?" as if an answer
were expected – and I painted on a large canvas. I
mean that I looked at the question in terms of the
whole Creation of which we are part, the Creation
which is still being made. I spoke of the way in
which God isn't making it all by Himself, but of
how He invites us to help make and re-make the
world in the shape of that which He had in mind
from the start, a world of hope and trust and love.
And when we do one little thing, however small,
which is unselfish and kind, we are doing just that –
putting ourselves on His side, working with Him on
a very longterm project. I find that an encouraging
idea: that however unimportant I am, however little
I seem to be able to do, the little I can do is part of

a much greater whole, and will never in the end be lost.

Of course, all this may not seem to add up to very much when we think of all the cruelty and suffering in the world, but the illustration of a hospital in time of war has helped me. There, men and women who have been wounded are looked after, and treated, and so far as possible helped to get better – for what? To be sent back to the war, and possibly for the same thing to happen all over again. But that possibility doesn't make doctors and nurses shrug their shoulders and ask, "What's the point?" The point stares them in the face: these are human beings who badly need medical attention, and so they give of their best. We may never know the practical outcome of what we do – but that's no cause for depression. It should remind us that when we make our small contribution of faith and hope and love, we are finally on the winning side, God's side if you like, even though we shall never see the end of the match! I quoted as an example the canteen lady who clears my table and cleans up after me, and who may find her job boring and unsatisfying; but she is still doing something which is of eternal worth. As the poet and hymn writer George Herbert put it:

> who sweeps a room as for Thy laws
> makes that and the action fine

I called on three witnesses in the programme. The first was Margaret, for whom life had become point-less when her daughter, Pam, had died four years previously. Pam was at university reading English, and Margaret had responded to her loss by, as it were, following in her footsteps, and studying English Literature at "O" and "A" Level. "I feel that I am doing what Pam would want me to do and not sit down and vegetate . . . And she was such a gentle soul and everybody loved her, that she would have wanted me to do something that was positive, and I feel I am doing that . . ."

Then there was Nina, a ballet dancer who became anorexic and who, when she started to come out of her illness thanks to a growing awareness of religious faith, responded by setting up an organization called Anorexic Aid, to bring together both anorexia sufferers and their families.

Finally there was Marie, who recounted her distress at trying to cope with her son's drug problem, but who found that day by day, through her rather unorthodox prayer life, she began to cope – providing it were only day by day!

It was largely, thus, through activity that these three people had come to terms with their feelings of pointlessness. But for some of us, it is precisely because we can't be busy like this that these feelings of emptiness and pointlessness come on. It is as if we have been in a fast-moving train with scenery flashing past, and the speed of the journey has borne us along. But now the train has stopped: previously the business of getting on with work, bringing up a family and so on, has absorbed us. Now it is gone. We are left alone with a feeling of emptiness and pointlessness. What then? I remembered how someone who was feeling empty inside described to me how she began to feel better when she really looked for the first time at the shapes and colours in the local park, the pattern of trees, and the sun playing through them on to the lake below. That is just one way to develop this still, rich centre within ourselves which doesn't depend on what is going on in the outside world. This has long been part of Christian tradition and is known as the contemplative way. It helps to put us, with all our fussing and anxieties, into perspective. And it was the early Christian Saint Augustine who put his finger on our feelings of emptiness and pointlessness when he said that we were all made for God Himself, and that our hearts are restless until they rest in Him. I finished the meditation by suggesting that He it is into whom we need to grow. If we really look, listen, love and care, we touch the hem of God's garment, and perhaps in time we shall come to see something of His face, His gaze, His love.

Our next meditation was on the subject of Handicap, but handicap which went beyond physical disability. We wanted to explore those things in our lives which frustrate us, and seem to rob the future of any hope. For instance, when we are tied by some physical illness, which may be chronic; when we have some emotional blockage which prevents us from making friends; when we seem to be imprisoned at home, looking after a sick or elderly relative; or tied in a boring, monotonous job from which there seems little or no escape; or even tied without any job at all, and few prospects of finding one. And the situation is made worse, because so few seem to understand the extent of our difficulty and frustration.

I started the exploration by recalling a television play I had seen, in which a doctor said that he often wished that there were no illness in the world, that we were born, went through life without difficulty,

and then died without any fuss. Now, apart from
the fact that he would presumably be out of a job,
it would also surely mean that we were living in a
totally different world from that in which we have
been put. For, as I see it, the world is, and always
has been, a world of struggle, struggle against the
natural forces of the world, to make life ordered and
civilization a possibility; struggle against physical
disease; struggle against all those limitations and
frustrations which prevent us from leading happy
and useful lives. Struggle, I believe, is at the heart
of the universe: that is how God made it. And I see
struggle clearly in the life of Jesus, not only in His
ministry, but also as a young man. We often forget
that He spent at least five times as long as a carpenter
as He did in preaching and teaching, and that meant
that He probably underwent most of the difficulties
associated with the job: fatigue, tiresome customers,
days when He was possibly unemployed, and other
anxieties. Throughout His ministry, whenever He
came across sickness, sadness or sin, He was always
ready to struggle against them. And in the Garden of
Gethsemane, He struggled against His natural desire
to save Himself from the dark event of Good Friday:
"Father, if it be Thy will, let this cup pass from me.
Nevertheless, not as I will, but as Thou wilt."

Most of the qualities we detect in other people –
courage, nobility, self-sacrifice, great-heartedness –
come from struggle. Through all the pains of growth
and struggle we are becoming more mature human
beings. And our present pain, difficulties and frustrations can help us do just that. So, when we become a
little detached from all our handicaps we can perhaps
see them in a different and more positive light.

There is another way too of looking at our frustrations, other than struggling against them. When struggling becomes useless and fruitless, there is a way of accepting them, which isn't just giving up or resigning ourselves to them, but seeing them as possible sources of good. Once we accept our limitations positively, then very often new possibilities open up to us. As the prayer puts it, "God grant us the courage to change what can be changed and to accept that which cannot be changed – and the wisdom to know the difference".

I recalled that one of the most wonderful human beings I have ever known was a Roman Catholic lady who had lain on a stretcher bed all her life, and who had to have everything done for her. But she was the one to whom other people, and especially young people, came, not to cheer her up, but to receive from her her wisdom and strength. She had learnt so well to live positively within the limitations which her handicap imposed.

Christine Smith is another example: she tells the story of her experience of the grim wasting disease of Muscular Dystrophy, in her book called *Clouds Got in my Way*.[3] To write the book she learnt to operate a tape recorder with her mouth. Looking back over the years, she concludes that she has been very fortunate. Her sense of humour has helped, and she says that she and her parents laughed out loud when they realized that she could easily be mistaken for Kermit the Frog in the Muppet Show! It was one sentence in her book which stood out for me, and which we then used as the thought for the week stemming from this programme: "Inside every disabled person, there is a beautiful butterfly struggling to get out." Christine seemed not only to live within the limitations imposed on her – but to see well beyond those limitations to the essential person inside.

Three people were able to testify from their own personal experience of what I was trying to say: Jackie, an agoraphobic, who was helped by a man who had the gift of spiritual healing; Jack, who had developed spondylitis at the age of twenty-three, and who had come to accept his physical frustrations (with difficulty) through turning his energies outward and working for disabled people in Remploy; and Loretta, a depressive for many years, who had found the greatest gift of all, a soul-mate, to whom she was able to hold on, however badly she felt.

Dietrich Bonhoeffer, the Lutheran pastor who died at the hands of a hangman in a Gestapo prison in 1945, just before the war ended, really had the last word, a word that came out of the heart of suffering and frustration:

> We must always lie close to the purpose of God, for that is nearness to life; and then nothing is impossible for all things are possible with God; no earthly power can touch us without His will, and danger can only drive us closer to Him. We can claim nothing for ourselves, and yet we may pray for everything. Our joy is hidden in suffering, our life in death . . .[4]

What is it that we all have, which we do not often talk about and yet which we feel most deeply? One answer to that question must be our guilt. Guilt was

87

our fourth exploration. Of course it is a good thing that we can feel guilty. Suppose you say something to a friend, and as soon as you have said it you know you have hurt them very much. You feel guilty and it is your guilt which moves you to say you are sorry and to stop the hurt from going any further. So a proper feeling of guilt is a good thing, and can be something very positive if we act on it. It can make us responsible in our relationships with other people, and prompts us to be reconciled with those we have hurt by our own thoughtlessness and carelessness.

If we get to the point of not recognizing at all when we have hurt anybody, and of never feeling guilty, then we are in trouble! It is that sort of insensitivity which is responsible for many of the world's miseries and cruelties. But there is a more insidious twist to guilt still. Many of us feel as if it isn't only other people whom we have hurt but God Himself (even though we may not express it like that). Deep in our subconscious lies this concept of an angry God, only waiting to catch us out and condemn us – and then our guilt breeds a sense of rejection and self-hatred.

However, none of this picture of an angry, condemnatory God stems from the New Testament, as Jesus depicted Him, for instance, in the well-known parable of the Prodigal Son. What has always struck me about that parable is the way in which the father doesn't wait for the son to make his prepared speech about being sorry: it was sufficient for him to see that his son was back again, so he immediately ran to embrace him, and give him the warmest of welcomes. That is the picture of God's welcome to us, as soon as we turn to Him. There He is, waiting to meet us, embrace us, welcome us home, ready to put things right for us.

The seventeenth-century poet George Herbert draws out that picture of God we have in the parable and takes it further.

> Love bade me welcome; yet my soul drew back,
>> Guiltie of dust and sinne,
> But quick-ey'd Love, observing me grow slack
>> From my first entrance in,
> Drew nearer to me, sweetly questioning
>> If I lack'd any thing.
>
> "A guest," I answer'd, "worthy to be here."
>> Love said, "You shall be he."
> "I the unkinde, ungrateful? Ah, my deare,
>> I cannot look on thee."
> Love took my hand, and smiling did reply,
>> "Who made the eyes but I?"
>
> "Truth Lord, but I have marr'd them: let my shame
>> Go where it doth deserve."
> "And know you not", sayes Love, "who bore the blame?"
>> "My deare, then I will serve."
> "You must sit down", sayes Love, "and taste my meat."
>> So I did sit and eat.[5]

But this feeling of guilt can be more insidious still, as the poet John Donne helps us to see:

> Wilt thou forgive that sin where I begun,
> Which was my sin, though it were done before?

Wilt thou forgive that sin through which I run
And so run still, though still I do deplore?
When thou hast done, thou hast not done
For I have more.

Wilt thou forgive that sin which I have won
Others to sin, and made my sin their door?
Wilt thou forgive that sin which I did shun
A year or two, but wallowed in a score?
When thou hast done, thou hast not done:
For I have more.[6]

Those four words "For I have more" say it all.
It sometimes feels as though we are carrying guilt
around with us like a leaden weight in our pocket,
even when we can't point to anything definite about
which we need to feel guilty. I quoted the curious
case of the lady who confessed to me that she felt
guilty, even though she did not seem to have anything to be guilty about! Guilt often seems connected
with what we *are*, rather than what we have *done* – or
even with *who* we are – and for none of this perhaps
can we really be blamed! Guilt is as perverse and as
real as that. It has been suggested that more than
half the beds in our mental hospitals are occupied
by those who have an over-loaded sense of guilt: it
is as potent as that.

Enough diagnosis! The question I wanted to ask
was, where do we find help in order to let its leaden
weight drop away? There are of course those of us
who find release in the ministrations of the Church
and especially the Sacrament of Confession – but I
have to say that the role of the Church so far as
guilt is concerned is ambivalent. It almost seems

to be as good at creating guilt as it is at releasing people from guilt. Sometimes, too, the Church, unconsciously, creates guilt simply by being there . . . I recall regularly meeting on my way to early morning service in the parish of Stretford a lady making for the train. After we had exchanged polite "Good Mornings" for about nine months, she stopped me one morning and said that she wished she didn't meet me, since every time she did she felt so guilty! "All you do is smile and say Good Morning – and I feel terrible!" What she was really saying was that the Church had made her feel guilty if she did not go regularly, and that, as she explained, was impossible at present because of her domestic circumstances.

Anne was the first person to be interviewed on the programme. She had had the devastating experience of her best friend's suicide eighteen months previously. The night before her suicide, the friend had phoned Anne about the possibility of sharing a flat together, which they had previously discussed on the advice of her psychiatrist. But Anne had, as she said, gone off the idea, thinking that she wasn't up to making that sort of sacrifice to look after her friend all the time. So she deliberately stalled on any decision, and said she would ring her friend the following evening – which was, of course, too late. That afternoon, her friend had killed herself. Anne was left, like many relatives and friends of suicide victims, feeling terribly guilty because she had failed her best friend. The last words they had had together were about a misunderstanding and were not words of love or encouragement. In the end, only one thing helped her: her belief in a God of love, a belief that she had throughout her life, but which had never before been so severely tested. Now she found that "this is the only thing that can give meaning to this absurd situation . . . If I can still believe that there is a God who is love even in this situation, then that is the only thing I can hold on to . . ."

Roger and Bernadette, parents of two spastic boys, my next two "witnesses" in the programme, spoke movingly about the insidious nature of guilt. Not only did they feel guilty themselves, and wondered whether it was something they had done or not done that had made the boys so handicapped, but other people also tried to make them feel guilty. They were, they said, being punished for their sins. What helped them to come to terms with their guilt wasn't anything very big or revolutionary, but a simple poem which they were given called "God's special Child". It made Roger and Bernadette see that they had done nothing to cause their children's handicap, but it went further still. It said that they had been specially chosen to look after the children. How ironic and what a judgement it was that a few anonymous written words accomplished more for those parents than the personal words of those who knew them!

It is being able to share guilt with someone whom we can trust which is likely to bring us most relief. Perhaps many of us hug our guilt to ourselves, because we are deeply afraid that if we shared it like this they'd cease to have a good impression of us, or even cease to love us. That is odd, if you think about it, since we all to some degree experience this guilt. And after all, we shall have more confidence knowing that they too, are people who struggled, and are struggling, with matters still unresolved in their own lives. I am not suggesting that we should parade or wallow in our guilt – but I am suggesting that we should always allow our guilt to be brought out into the open in the presence of a trusted friend and for that guilt to be shared. We shall never be healthy or healed until the poison of guilt has been allowed to drain away.

There is one last verse in the poem of John Donne which offers a resolution of the guilt expressed in the first two verses:

> I have a sin of fear, that when I've spun
> My last thread, I shall perish on the shore;
> But swear by thyself that at my death thy Son
> Shall shine as he shines now and heretofore:
> And having done that, thou hast done:
> I fear no more.

Our next and last exploration in the series provoked some disagreement amongst us as advisers. Could we, should we try to cover the subject of the fear of ageing and dying? Would it not be just too much for our viewers, especially for the aged themselves? The doubters lost the argument – and to judge from the response to the programme they were wrong. As we shall see later, the volume of response to this programme was greater than to any other in this series.

I felt that the programme might prove helpful if we were able to get our viewers to bring out and look at their half-buried fears on the subject. For obviously, the more we push such fears away, the more control they take over us and the greater the psychological damage they'll do to us. It is perspective we need. I started by suggesting that there is a proper rhythm in life, like the seasons of the year – and that each season has its compensations and its sadnesses. The trouble is that, awkward creatures that we are, we always think that to be in the next or the last stage is better than where we are now. For instance, it is difficult when we are older to remember clearly the agonies we went through when we were growing up: our shyness and awkwardness, our fear of being thought different from other people, and so on. So we put on our rose-coloured spectacles, and think that all was perfect in the golden days of youth. And we are not helped by all those advertisements which invite us to buy some pill or cream which will make us "look younger", "feel younger" – and worst of all, "stay younger", as if the one crime were not to be young. But not to be young has its compensations: the experiences you had, the memories you gain, the satisfaction you can enjoy perhaps of work well done and difficulties you have overcome. So many things that were desperately important to us when we were young seem to matter very little when age begins to take over. We seem to gain a lot of perspective. And of course, it isn't necessarily downhill all the way: for many people there are still many things they want to do. As the poet Longfellow has it:

It is too late! Ah, nothing is too late
Till the tired heart shall cease to palpitate.
Chaucer, at Woodstock with the nightingales,
At sixty wrote the *Canterbury Tales*:

Goethe at Weimar, toiling to the last,
Completed *Faust* when eighty years were past.
These are indeed exceptions: but they show
How far the gulf-stream of our youth may flow
Into the arctic regions of our lives . . .
For age is opportunity no less
Than youth itself, though in another dress
And as the evening twilight fades away
The sky is filled with stars, invisible by day . . .[7]

I have often thought that the life of Jesus illustrates
that which we take too often for granted: as if it's
length of years rather than quality of life which matters. He did not live to be a man of ripe old age –
and yet, although He died at the age of thirty-three,
most of us feel that there was a completeness and
fulfilment in His life which no amount of increasing
years could really improve on. What matters in our
lives is not how long they are, but of what sort they
are. It is sad to see how many older characters seem
not only to have stopped growing as human beings,
but to have become hard and inflexible, their worst
traits emphasized. In other words, we could die at
thirty and show all the signs of being mature; we
can live until we are ninety and never really grow
up and become mature. One of the letters of St
Paul uses this word "mature" in connection with
Jesus, and says that our goal as human beings
is to reach "mature manhood, measured by nothing less than the full stature of Christ". That is,
whether we are young or old, it is how we are
portraying to others what Christ was and is, which
counts.

Naturally, one reason why we fear growing old

is because it means that death may be just around the corner. In different ways in my life I have lived with death close at hand, and far from finding it gloomy and morbid, I think that it has made my life richer. I have already described how my pilot and I were shot down off the west coast of Greece in 1943, and came within thirty seconds of death. Then, I had a narrow escape with a heart attack seven or eight years ago. Both these incidents have made me realize in a curious way that coming close to the boundary of death makes us appreciate life more and makes every day more worthwhile. If life just went on and on, without the boundary of death, it would lose a sense of purpose and meaning, and become much more trivial. So I believe, from my own experience, that the boundary of death is not just an enemy to be feared, but in God's time – not ours – to be accepted. And to be seen as a blessing rather than as a curse. This is what Dr Glin Bennett has to say on the subject in his book *Patients and Their Doctors*.

> Those who have in any way come close to death thereafter speak in a special way about life, and manage to live life fully . . . taking each day as it comes. I would find it hard to savour the richness of summer without reference to the winter that preceded it and which will follow it. Day would be hard to imagine without night. As I become aware of death because I am getting older and encounter more people who are dying, so life becomes richer. This is not because each

day I move nearer to the end of my life but rather because the reality of death intensifies the reality of living.[8]

I have often spoken with patients, especially in hospices, who have been given a short time in which to live. And what has always impressed me is the way in which some of them say that it is as if they have woken up for the first time and generally become more aware, so that despite their pain and discomfort, they have found life to be more worthwhile, and every day important.

One of the endearing features about all those I interviewed in this programme was that none of them found the prospect of death easy to visualize, and were very honest about their fears, and what they thought would happen if and when they got to Heaven! Marie, in particular, intrigued us. I asked her whether she was looking forward to being re-united with her husband, and this is how the conversation proceeded from there.

> Yes, very much so, but I'm a bit bothered about what we will all look like and whether we will all recognize each other. Now, for example, my parents died a long, long time ago when I was only a child. If I died now would they recognize me as I am now or even with a glorified body, whatever that will be, and will I recognize them? This bothers me. And of course there are certain people that I may not want to meet in the next world because, being a human being, at the moment there are, well, I would say three

people I have met and that I don't ever want
to see again.

They've hurt you, you mean?

Yes. And I don't think that I'll ever want to
see them in the next world and I'm worried
about that.

You find it difficult to forgive them?

I suppose that's something in me. I don't
know that it's the forgiving, it's the for-
getting part. I suppose you can sort of key
yourself up to forgive things but you can't
always forget them. I'm afraid I'm the sort
of person that can't forget but I suppose in
the next world our faculties will be different.

*So in a way you're hoping that you won't
have eyes in the next world in order to be
able to see them?*

Yes, I'm wondering about that, I'm wondering just what our bodies are going to be
like.

*Well, we shall not know yet awhile, shall
we?*

If we are going to overcome our fear of ageing
and dying, I think that one thing is essential: that
we accept, acknowledge and come to terms with
those experiences of loss we have throughout our
lives. Even in those circumstances which seem to be
opportunities for celebration, like leaving school, or
marriage, or becoming a parent, there is, of course,
some loss. And if you want to take it further back
still, when we are born, we lose the warmth and

98

security of our mother's womb. Gain and loss – but also loss and gain. To come to accept our dying and death is to accept loss; it is also to be opened up to a new hope of joy in eternal life.

This hope of loss and gain together is affirmed in two pieces of literature we used in the programme. The first was by Henry Scott Holland, Canon of St Paul's at the beginning of this century. Perhaps there is a slight feeling of sentimentality about these words, but the naturalness of the continuing relationship between two people beyond death is so well expressed, and his words have obviously meant a lot to many bereaved people.

> Death is nothing at all. I have only slipped away into the next room. I am I and you are you. Whatever we were to each other, that we are still. Call me by my old familiar name, speak to me the easy way you always used, put no difference in your tone, wear no forced air of solemnity or sorrow, laugh as we always laughed at the little jokes we enjoyed together. Play, smile, think of me, pray for me. Let my name be ever the household word it always was, let it be spoken without an effort, without the ghost of a shadow on it. Life means all that it ever meant. It is the same as it ever was; there is absolutely unbroken continuity. Why should I be out of mind because I am out of sight? What is this death but a negligible accident? I am but waiting for you, for an interval, somewhere very near, just around the corner. All is well. Thanks to God.[9]

The second was a prayer found in Father Bede Jarrett's prayer book after his death, which contained these unforgettable words:

> . . . And Life is eternal, and Love is immortal, and death is only a horizon, and an horizon is nothing save the limit of our sight . . .[10]

If you look at what Jesus has to say in the New Testament you do not find any detailed descriptions of the after life: there was a certain reticence about His words here as elsewhere. There is a Mystery about life and death and after life, which we must always cherish. We must live with that Mystery — but always in confidence.

> What Jesus said about becoming as little children and taking no thought for the morrow applies with special force to our future in and beyond the grave. We live now from hour to hour, from minute to minute, as those who are ever receiving from the unknown, and that is all we need to know. Ours can be the confidence of a child living in his father's house whose needs are supplied as, and only as, they arise . . .
>
> With regard to all the deaths we have to die, including the final death of the grave, we must always remember that sufficient unto the day is the evil thereof and that as our days are so shall our strength be. If we are like little children we shall not worry

about what is going to happen next year or
even tomorrow.[11]

Audience research is always to be treated with cau-
tion because of the smallness of the research sample
taken, and because such a sample doesn't tell us anything about the concentration of the people who have
their sets switched on! But the audience research
covering the last three programmes in the series of
six was encouraging. There was an average audience
of 600,000 people, which is very small in comparison
with Coronation Street ratings but significant, we
thought, in terms of the number of individuals whom
we were addressing. Numbers of viewers increased
over the three programmes, and by the end of the
final programme something like 3.1 million people
had seen at least part of the meditation trilogy.
Research also showed that viewers of the meditations
tended to be older and more down-market than the
average ITV viewer: 69 per cent fell into the category
of semi-skilled and unskilled manual worker, and the
unemployed. This is particularly interesting, in view
of the criticisms often levelled at the way in which
the Church only provides for the middle classes. All
three programmes showed an Appreciation Index of
something just under 80, which category is described
as "very interesting, and/or enjoyable".

Two-thirds of those questioned said that they
themselves or someone in the household had chosen to watch: more than half claimed to have found
the programme helpful; over a quarter felt a desire
to speak to someone about the content of the programme; and about half had found the programme
a "pleasant change"(!) from the usual Sunday outside

broadcast service. We were reassured by the fact that more than a third disagreed that the series had been boring or difficult to follow! One letter we received said that the programmes were depressing, and one that they made the viewer miserable. I guess that you can't win them all over! Several letters had appreciated the "unhurried tempo, giving time to meditate and absorb the message" and the way in which it was "sincere, humble and caring". "I felt more drawn to God than in any church", wrote a lady from Broadstairs. "If only religion could be explained in this way more often", wrote a gentleman from Bristol. "Moving, uplifting and wonderfully reassuring", wrote a lady from Palmers Green, London, and an anonymous writer described the programme as a "quiet, inspiring union with God". "Sensitive, thoughtful and caring", wrote a lady from St Albans, and one writer delighted us by saying that although she had been moved to tears, she was "not distressed and at the end felt nourished" – for spiritual nourishment is precisely what we were aiming at.

The Air Care phone-in system offered after the series of programmes was only to those viewers in Granadaland. We had as our background support system thirty-seven clergymen and ministers covering different localities in the region who were very willing to respond to any obvious need in their own area and to act as general "resource persons" for us. The twelve counsellors ready to receive the calls came from the Family Care Line service sponsored by the National Children's Home, and attached to Piccadilly Radio. Most of the calls we received were from people who simply wished to talk about their particular experience of the subject the programme was exploring – or about other sad experiences they had suffered. It was the patient, listening ear that mattered.

The numbers of phone calls after each programme weren't large, amounting to just over two hundred in all, with about twice as many letters. But too often the official criterion of success in programmes such as this is simply taken to be the number of people who call, rather than the reasons for the call and the way in which the call is dealt with. I can illustrate this well from the programme we did on guilt. The average length of call was thirty-five minutes: clearly, it was a painful subject, in which people needed time to develop the confidence in order to speak of it at all. And one call lasted one hour thirty-five minutes. Then, one man was able, through the anonymity of the phone, to deliver himself of a piece of guilt about a certain incident that had happened thirty-four years previously, and of which he had never been able to speak before. I visited him the following week, and the release he had enjoyed had begun to make all the difference to his life. Some of us felt that the whole system of Air Care had justified itself simply on the basis of that one man's experience, even if it had proved the only phone call to be received that morning. A statistic of one can be as significant as a statistic of one hundred, if we are not beguiled by the crude criterion of numbers. And such a crude criterion is always inadmissible when we are dealing with the cares and anxieties of real people. One of the most welcome letters we received spoke of the way in which the writer felt as if the programme "was devised for me alone" – and that expressed our hope perfectly.

CHAPTER NINE

***

Remembering

We were fortunate in that our next series of meditations fell on the first three Sundays of November 1986, and so the subjects almost chose themselves, for the first Sunday was All Souls Day, and the second was Remembrance Day. Consequently, the overall title of the series was "Remembering".

In the first programme, we looked at good memories, especially of relatives and friends who have died. Our counsellors were delighted that we were to explore a happy subject for a change! Our second meditation led us to those who lost their lives not only in the two World Wars, but also in Northern Ireland and the Falkland Islands. On the third Sunday, we explored the dark side of our personal remembering: past hurts we have inflicted on others and the hurts others have inflicted on us. The ingredients of the programme were roughly the same, with St Ann's Choir and Peter Barkworth as the reader, and they were filmed at Capesthorne Hall, a stately home in Cheshire, with spacious grounds and gardens, which gave some superb backgrounds for quiet reflection – even if rhododendrons in full bloom may have looked a little incongruous when the programmes were transmitted in a wet November!

I introduced the general theme of remembering

by noticing the statistic that every year we buy more birthday, anniversary and Christmas cards, and that we have cards for those occasions when we have forgotten to remember. But of course, the business of remembering goes far beyond our friends' birthdays. To be able to remember the whole kaleidoscope of people and events that has made up our lives is really what keeps us human. And it may be that being able to remember and reflect on the past, and being able to look forward to the future, is that which chiefly distinguishes us from the animal kingdom. If we could not remember we should lose the precious sense of who we are: our personalities and our remembering are all bound up together.

We looked at good times in the past: those events which have given us joy and pleasure, occasions when things all seem to have come together and there has been a sense of rightness about everything. The writer and dramatist J. B. Priestley, in a short piece called *Delight*, painted a heart-warming picture of "family silliness, domestic clowning". He pictures a fairly large family:

> You start with any bit of nonsense, usually at the dining table, and then everybody adds shaggy pieces of their own, until the whole table is roaring and screaming and the scarlet cheeks of the younger children are wet with tears of laughter . . . and it is scenes like this, without dignity, real wit or beauty, made up of screeching and bellowing and fourth-rate jokes about treacle pudding or castor oil, that a man who feels his life ebbing out may recall with an anguish of

regret and tenderness, remembering as if it were a lost bright kingdom of the family all at home and being silly . . .[1]

Monica, our first person to be interviewed, looked back at her happily married life until her husband had died six months previously. She said that although there were ups and downs in their, as in most other, marriages, she could talk with great joy about it. That which had given her most joy and happiness was the day when, after eight years' struggle and hard work, they had eventually managed to get their mentally handicapped son Steven into the home where he now was. She concluded by saying that it was the very difficulties in their lives which had drawn them closer and made their life together one which was "both exciting and challenging and happy".

For Margaret, our second "witness", it was the small things which mattered and brought her so much happy "remembering".

The first week of my married life was a shock because I suddenly realized that I was tied down, but after getting used to that, it was one long and happy experience of contentment. You know, I remember tiny things like being at home doing something as mundane as the ironing and it might be one of his shirts and I'd suddenly take off and waltz around the room with it. It was like that. Or he'd come home and I'd be rushing about going on about all the things that I hadn't managed to get done that day and he'd say: "It doesn't matter, love." He used to ring during the day just to say "hello". It was really happiness and as the years go by, you don't remember particular events, things seem to merge into one.

I even remember his last days with a smile. He had cancer and the drugs he was on distorted his speech. He and Mum irritated one another. Anyway, he was in the downstairs room and in spite of not being well he was drawing a plan for a feeding method for a hutch of rabbits. Mum was making an enormous attempt to be pleasant and he was attempting to explain the plan to her but she couldn't understand what he was saying. Anyway, he said something and Mum tried to interpret it. She said, "Are you saying 'sick'? Do you mean 'sick'?" We were sitting by the fire and suddenly I knew what he was trying to tell her with such energy. I was scared that it would suddenly click with Mum and we were soon all in giggles because no one dared put Mum in her place. What he was actually saying was: "You're thick." And then it dawned on Mum and she too burst out laughing.

What is the connection between such memories and religious faith? Unlikely as it seems, those memories relate directly to the New Testament view of eternal life. We often think of eternal life as meaning, quite simply, continued existence beyond the grave. But although it includes the idea of duration, it denotes a quality of life which starts here and now in the midst of our ordinary, everyday experiences. St John says that God has given us eternal life, and its possibility is ours already. So in the happy memories we are exploring, we have hints of that eternal life, when we are in harmony with other people and feel right with the Universe. We only have glimpses now, broken bits and pieces, you might say, glimpses of that which we will enjoy to the full in the hereafter. But those glimpses are just sufficient to help us see that eternal life isn't remote from our daily existence, and it is closely related to our remembering. Related, too, to the day on which the programme was being transmitted: All Souls Day, which despite its rather chilling title, simply encourages us to say "thank you" for all those ordinary people who have had a good deal of often unconscious influence on us for good. Joyce Grenfell, in her autobiography, *Joyce Grenfell Requests the Pleasure*, recalls her mother in a very human way:

> She has been gone for twenty-two years but the qualities that drew people to her still ring in the air like music for those who knew and loved her; and they are many. The patterns she made on the memory are clear, funny, exasperating, lovable. Her weaknesses brought pain, but her essence, and this is what has endured, is light, luminous and illuminating.

She found it difficult to describe her mother physically, as she said,

> It's no good. I can't get her into focus

that way. Perhaps her legs may help. She was always proud of them; well-shaped with pretty ankles and neat narrow feet. The last time she was in England, a year before she died at sixty-five, she was walking across Grosvenor Square near the U.S. Embassy and an American sailor wolf-whistled at her from behind. She was pleased about this. "I'm afraid you're fifty years too late." "No, ma'am," said the sailor, "it's never too late with legs like those."[2]

So human – and yet a lovely remembering, a bringing in to the present of someone who meant so much to her.

The Church has a daily celebration through which it remembers and brings into the present the life, death and resurrection of Jesus, and so at the conclusion of each of our meditations in this series we looked at one aspect of the service of Holy Communion. "Do this in remembrance of me", He said, and whether it is done with great splendour in a Cathedral, or very simply in an individual's sick room, the response and the remembrance are the same. The celebration goes back to the Upper Room the night before Jesus was crucified, where He shared His last supper with His friends, and tried to help them see the inner meaning of what was going to happen to Him.

Now to do something in remembrance of someone has more meaning than just thinking of them. That is why we like to send birthday cards, put flowers on Mother's grave, plan a garden of remembrance. So what were the friends of Jesus to remember as they did this in remembrance of Him? Most chiefly, His goodness, for what the Prayer Book calls "our creation, preservation and all the blessings of this life". There are many names for this service of Holy Communion: the Lord's Supper; the Breaking of Bread; the Mass; and one of the names is the Eucharist, which simply means thanksgiving, and thanksgiving, in particular, for all the occasions of memories which have given us so much happiness.

Our second meditation in this series couldn't help but revive personal and poignant memories for some viewers, since it was transmitted on Remembrance Day. I tried to symbolize all these memories by sketching in my own memory of David, in the Second World War, a member of the University Air Squadron with me, and enlisted in the RAF on the same day as I was. Like me, he too came to the conclusion (rightly or wrongly) that however beastly war was, to let Nazism go unchecked would be an even worse evil. But he often used to read Wilfred Owen's First World War poems, to remind himself that the glamour of being an Air Force Pilot shouldn't blind him to the real horror of it all.

What candles may be held to speed them all?
Not in the hands of boys, but in their eyes
Shall shine the holy glimmer of good-byes . . .[3]

Like Wilfred Owen, David was killed in action. And yet although it was forty-five years since I had last seen him, I could still vividly recall his handsome features, his humorous expressions, his youthful high hopes for a better world when the war was over.

Then of course, in our own decade, there are those who have been killed in the Falklands War. David Tinker was one of them: he was serving on *HMS Glamorgan* when it was hit by an Exocet missile. Here is part of a letter he wrote to his father:

> I suppose this is all an experience one should go through if only to drive home for each generation how stupid war is. Certainly the trivia of life and the important things are all brought to mind by this. And how much the trivia are at the forefront of normal life and the important things put away, or not done, or left to do later and then forgotten. Here, certainly, the material things are unimportant, and "human things", values and ways of life are thought about by everybody.[4]

What a curiously ironic and tragic comment on human nature that it should take a major crisis like a war to restore a sense of perspective in human affairs . . .

One of those I interviewed in the programme, Donald, who was taken prisoner by the Japanese at seventeen years of age when *HMS Exeter* was sunk in the Java Sea, made the same point. "Being a prisoner", he said, "changed me. Things which you thought important previously became unimportant. I think you tend to care less about material things. When you are reduced to nothing, when you have got nothing, absolutely nothing, then nothing seems to matter except food and keeping alive."

Of course, many in my generation are very often

nostalgic about the Second World War. Not only when we tell our tales about it and perhaps bore other people, but also when we sit glued to our TV screens watching those old wartime films which seem to come around with endless repetition. But it isn't only nostalgia: it is something to do with the way in which, during the war, many people found themselves more alive. Everything was so much more vital; we were devoted to a common goal and purpose which we had never found in peacetime. There was a support, sharing and neighbourliness which is only apparent today when some tragedy or disaster occurs. And there were also opportunities for daring, adventure and heroism in the war that we seem to lack in our cushioned society. Along with all that, some seemed to reach a potential in themselves which pointed them further to the stars. Here is a poem written by an American pilot, John Gillespie Magee, serving with the Royal Canadian Air Force, who was killed in action in December 1941 at the age of nineteen. He became so excited after his first flight in a Spitfire that he wrote this poem literally on the back of an envelope:

Oh, I have slipped the surly bonds of earth
And danced the skies on laughter-silvered wings;
Sunward I've climbed, and joined the tumbling
  mirth
Of sun-split clouds – and done a hundred things
You have not dreamed of – wheeled and soared
  and swung
High in the sunlit silence. Hov'ring there,
I've chased the shouting wind along, and flung
My eager craft through footless halls of air.

Up, up the long, delirious, burning blue
I've topped the windswept heights with easy
   grace
Where never lark, nor even eagle flew.
And, while with silent, lifting mind I've trod
The high untrespassed sanctity of space,
Put out my hand, and touched the face of God.[5]

I remember reading one of the wreaths left at the foot
of the Cenotaph after the Second World War which
simply had attached to it five words: "Not in vain,
my darling." Now was that just loving sentiment, or
was it the truth? And if it were the truth, in what
sense was it so? I tried to make the point that since
human welfare and progress seem in great part to
depend upon our willingness to sacrifice ourselves,
of course it was the truth, even when the results of
that self-sacrifice seem so meagre. But I believe that
it is the truth in another sense, too. Although in the
meditations we were thinking about *our* remembering, I believe that God remembers too. Often, we
picture Him as a stern, unbending character who
merely and passively observes the scene of His
creation, and is totally unmoved by it. The modern
biologist, Charles Birch, paints a slightly different
picture:

> The main line of Christian theology has
> held to the belief that God cannot suffer,
> or otherwise change. But the idea of God
> as responsive to suffering is a theme which
> can be found in Hebrew thought, all the way
> from Genesis to Paul.[6]

113

God is affected, that is, by all that happens in His own creation, from the tiny generous action of a small boy or girl to a martyr's sacrifice. As one philosopher put it, the image we should have of Him is that of "a tender care that nothing be lost". "The merest puff of existence is not without its significance to God", he said. "A tender care that nothing be lost": there, then, is God, Himself, remembering, and treasuring all that is noble, sacrificial and worthwhile – even when, humanly speaking, all these qualities seem to achieve little or nothing.

So the answer to the question we naturally and tenderly ask about someone we hold dear, and whose life was tragically cut short by the war, "Was it in vain?", is "No, not in vain", even when we are feeling the loss most keenly. All is saved in God's experience, and the ocean of His experience is the experience of all that is of value, even the tiniest loving thought. Norman Pittenger, in his book *Picturing God*, puts it like this:

> Whatever good we have known, which is to say, whatever bits of heaven have been part of our experience, whatever has been significant and valuable in our lives, whatever has been done or thought or said which is a contribution to the "love that moves the sun and the other stars": all this God keeps in His heart and cherishes.[7]

Despite all that I have said previously about hymns, there is curiously one verse of a hymn, by Timothy Rees, "God is Love", which perfectly expresses the thought that God is affected by us and suffers with us.

And when human hearts are breaking
under sorrow's iron rod,
There they find that self-same aching
deep within the heart of God.

One incident in the war stands out very clearly
in my mind. It was Christmas 1944, five months
before the war ended in Germany. Things were
at their roughest in our prisoner-of-war camp in
Saxony. There was terrible overcrowding, since the
Ardennes offensive had resulted in more prisoners
being taken than could be coped with. Shortage and
sharing of bunks meant that we slept two nights out
of every three. Food was scarce, to say the least,
because our bombing had dislocated German transport, and no Red Cross parcels were getting to us
from Switzerland. Mail from home barely trickled
through, and the end of the war seemed as far away
as ever. The prospect for our Christmas dinner was
sauerkraut and more sauerkraut – and that was
considered a luxury! So how was Christmas to be
Christmas for us – as it was meant to be?

For some of us there had to be a public recognition
of a celebration of Christ's birth. After several rep-
resentations to the German Commandant, we were
allowed to have a service of midnight communion
in a freezing barrack-block, to and from which we
were marched by the German guards. The bread
we used in the service was hardly that which would
be used now in church: it was rye-bread which had
been sent to Rommel's Afrika Korps and returned to
Germany after his surrender. No wine, of course –
tea made of mint leaves was its substitute. But just

115

imagine the joy in sharing that service, still able to do this in remembrance of Him, and of His birth, in particular. It was the coming of Love in this loveless place and the sharing of that love with all those friends and relatives from whom we were physically separated, but with whom through that same love we were inextricably linked. Remembering, that is, the same Christ who, for love of us, sacrificed His own life, and looking to the same Christ for spiritual food and strength.

Our third and last meditation in this series centred on bad memories which still haunt us and have left their scar. How can these memories be healed?

I recalled that when I was seven years old, a very trivial thing happened to me, but it left a nasty scar and made me realize ever since how any act of injustice always rankles. I had been ill, and was sent for convalescence to stay with an aunt who lived in the Midlands. Without being unkind, a "battleaxe" would not be entirely inappropriate in trying to describe her. One night, when we had supper – meals were always very formal – my aunt had to leave the room for some reason. When she came back she accused me, quite unjustly, of helping myself to some Worcestershire sauce. No amount of pleading on my part would convince her she was wrong: small an incident as it was, the memory of such injustice has lingered on, as you can see, for sixty years afterwards. It made me conscious at quite a tender age of all the things that are done to us which perhaps we remember for the rest of our lives – and, of course, there are infinitely worse things than being falsely accused of taking some Worcestershire sauce. Ruth, for instance, one of those I interviewed in the programme, told of the way in which her husband had hurt her, always emotionally and sometimes physically, all the way through their married life.

If however we simply live with, and constantly re-live, hurts and grievances that have been done to us, then bitterness is almost certain to creep in, and we shall be tempted to behave in a hurtful way ourselves. Very often, the wounds we feel only result in our inflicting as many wounds as possible on other people – or, at least, of never letting them forget that our wounds hurt! Sometimes, of course, we react by making those wounds an excuse for not taking responsibility for our own lives. "Look what I've suffered since I was a child", we seem to say, "and I'm determined that the rest of the world will keep on paying for it. I'll make my sufferings the excuse." But there is another way and it goes back to the crucifixion story.

> And when they had come to the place called Calvary, there they crucified Him, and the criminals, one on the right hand and the other on the left.
> Then Jesus said, "Father, forgive them, for they do not know what they do." And they divided His garments and cast lots.

I think that one word describes well what Jesus did on the cross: the word "absorb". If I do you a mean action, you may well think you have to do me a mean action in return. The evil I started has won; it has produced more evil, and the damage is multiplied. But suppose that you meet my mean action patiently, and in a spirit of forgiveness. Then, the evil I have

117

started has lost: it has been cut short, absorbed by your goodness. Isn't the example of Jesus on the cross the perfect example of evil being absorbed by love? It would only have needed from Him one word of resentment or bitterness against His enemies, and everything that He was achieving by His death would have been wrecked. At the moment when the pain of crucifixion was at its worst, He prayed for those who had caused Him so much suffering: "Father, forgive them, for they do not know what they do."

That seems to me to point to the way in which we are to try to take on board all the hurts that are done to us, and stop their power to produce more hurts. When we assume responsibility like this, and refuse to shelter behind injustice and resentment, we give ourselves the chance to grow as human beings. Nothing blocks our growth more, or plays greater havoc with our lives, than nurturing the resentments that feed poison into every part of us. This necessity for absorption found perfect expression in a prayer I came across recently which was written by an unknown prisoner in Ravensbruck concentration camp, and left by the side of the body of a dead child.

> O Lord, remember not only the men and women of good will, but also those of ill will. But do not remember all the suffering they have inflicted on us; remember the fruits we have borne, thanks to this suffering – our comradeship, our loyalty, our humility, our caring, our generosity, the greatness of heart which has grown out of all this, and when they come to judgement let all the fruits which we have borne be their forgiveness.[8]

Of course, over and above what others do and have done to us, is what we have done (sometimes unconsciously) to others. I think that the worst dream I have relates to broken relationships in which I have been involved, even when I keep on convincing myself that the break did not happen just because of me! I have often dwelt on these broken relationships, re-lived the incidents which led to the break-up, and renewed the hurts which long ago should have been buried. It is the people involved in those hurts who have doubtless come back in my dreams and plagued me.

Jennifer, another lady I interviewed in the programme, recounted her painful memory of the way in which she had hurt her child. Her drinking had caused her, she said, to have that child: she was a Foetal Alcohol Syndrome baby and as a result is quite mentally handicapped.

> She will always be there as a reminder of what drinking, my drinking, resulted in for another human being, for my child . . . My other daughter also suffered as a result of my drinking, and I know the whole affair must have been a totally confusing and painful experience for her. Obviously, you can't put the clock back, but you do have to accept what has happened and come to terms with it . . . !

One way of coming to terms with it is through the new life and forgiveness generously given over and over again, more particularly at the celebration of

Holy Communion. John Wesley's diary draws out the connection between this forgiveness and Holy Communion in the entry he wrote for 3rd September 1739:

> I talked largely with my mother, who told me that, till a short time since, she had scarce heard such a thing mentioned as the having forgiveness of sins now or God's spirit bearing witness with her spirit; much less did she imagine that this was the common privilege of all true believers. "Therefore," said she, "I never darst ask it for myself. But two or three weeks ago, while my son Hall was pronouncing those words, in delivering the cup to me, 'The blood of our Lord Jesus Christ which was given for thee', the words struck through my heart, and I knew God, for Christ's sake, had forgiven *me* all *my* sins."[9]

All the hurts that we have suffered; all the hurts we have inflicted on others; all the sins which we can't remember – all these find release through the One who took upon Himself the burden of the world's sin, a living self-sacrifice which we recall week by week and day by day in the service of Holy Communion.

Not long ago, in Iran, a young man, the son of a Bishop, was brutally murdered. Here is a prayer which the Bishop offered after it happened, and it seems to sum up beautifully all that we had been struggling to express in this meditation:

We remember not only our son but also
  his murderers;
Not because they killed him in the prime
of his youth and made our hearts bleed and
our tears flow.
Not because with this savage act they have
brought further disgrace on the name of our
country among the civilized nations of the
  world;
But because through their crime we now
follow thy footsteps more closely in the way
  of sacrifice.
The terrible fire of this calamity burns up
all selfishness and possessiveness in us;
Its flame reveals the depth of depravity
and meanness and suspicion, the dimension
of hatred and the measure in sinfulness in
human nature;
It makes obvious as never before our need
to trust in God's love as shown in the cross
of Jesus and His resurrection;
Love which makes us free from hate towards
our persecutors;
Love which brings patience, forbearance,
courage, loyalty, humility, generosity, greatness of heart;
Love which more than ever deepens our
trust in God's final victory and His eternal
designs for the Church and for the world;
Love which teaches us how to prepare ourselves to face our own day of death.
O God,
Our son's blood has multiplied the fruit
of the Spirit in the soil of our souls;

121

So when his murderers stand before Thee
on the day of judgement
Remember the fruit of the Spirit by which
they have enriched our lives.
And forgive.[10]

The viewing figures for this series of meditations
were interesting, going up from 600,000 in the first
programme to nearly three-quarters of a million in
the third. There was a trough in the middle, falling
to nearly 400,000 – but it was (we like to think!)
because simultaneously BBC 1 was transmitting the
traditional and popular Cenotaph service. More than
three-quarters of those interviewed indicated that
they "liked the programme format", and more than
half said that they would welcome another series.
We were further encouraged by some of the written
comments we had. "Some programmes seem nice
and superficial, yours was real and helpful", wrote a
Hampshire viewer. That pleased us: it is too easy for
religious programmes to be bland and to lack reality.
"It made compelling viewing: the sense of God's
presence lingers long after the programme finishes",
wrote a London couple. "God spoke strongly to me
during the programme and started a healing of bitterness in my heart", wrote a Yorkshire lady – and
that comment pleased us best, since something had
actually happened in her life, as a result of what it
was that we were trying to say and do.

We were able to offer a wider telephone system
of Air Care after this series of meditations, through
the operation of British Telecom's Link Line. This
enabled viewers, not only in the Granada region
but throughout the country, to phone simply at the

cost of a local call, Granada paying the difference. Family Care Line again provided the counsellors. Understandably, the greatest number of telephone calls and letters was after the third meditation, on bad memories, in which many viewers obviously wanted help in letting the healing process begin to do its work. Clearly the business of making personal contact with those who would benefit from such a thing was a much bigger task than when we offered the service in Granadaland only. But once again, we were much encouraged by the willingness of church representatives in particular to make themselves available for such help, and to respond to requests for personal visits. Once more we were able to see the value of co-operation between those of us working in the field of religious television and those in the ordinary day-to-day life of the Church.

CHAPTER TEN

Hope

The wheel comes full circle – and we arrive at the set of meditations which sparked off the phone call, with which the book opened. We filmed in Cartmel Priory, just eight hundred years old, and now a parish church in North Lancashire. The form of meditation was roughly similar to that of the previous series. Peter Barkworth was our reader, and a quartet from Grasmere and a student choir from Christ's and Notre Dame College, Liverpool, sang the hymns.

Since the meditations were due for transmission on the first three Sunday mornings in January 1988, the subject appropriate to New Year consideration readily presented itself: the subject of Hope. What hope was there for the world in 1988? Next, what hope was there for us, that living in a world full of violence and suffering we wouldn't become insensitive and dulled by it all? And then on the third Sunday, we were to explore what hope there was for us, that we should grow as human beings, that the New Year resolutions we made about "being better" wouldn't just fade away, forgotten.

So, first, what hope was there for the world? I tried to make the point to the viewers that whatever their present circumstances, however many anxieties they

had, it is impossible to live without hope. We seem
to act in hope most of our lives. It is not only that
which keeps people working for something better in
the future: it works on the ordinary level of life, too.
You wouldn't, for instance, book a holiday, take
trouble with your gardening or allotment, marry a
husband or wife, or bring children into the world,
unless you had some sort of hope. Hope, in other
words, is built into the fabric of our lives.

> Hope is the thing with feathers –
> That perches in the soul –
> And sings the tune without the words –
> And never stops – at all –
>
> And sweetest – in the gale – is heard –
> And sore must be the storm –
> That could abash the little Bird
> That kept so many warm –
>
> I've heard it in the chillest land –
> And on the strangest sea –
> Yet, never, in Extremity,
> It asked a crumb of Me.[1]

I like the line in that poem,

> And sweetest in the gale is heard

indicating how the bird of hope still goes on singing
in the midst of terribly adverse circumstances. Some
people we have all known still hope even when life is
at its roughest for them, and when many of the good
things we take for granted have been torn away from
them: families, friends, good health, enough money

and so on. I talked in the programme to Cyril who has been a victim of Multiple Sclerosis for twenty-three years, and found himself increasingly immobile, and I asked him what he was still hoping for – a cure? No, he said: what he really hoped for was to continue to be sustained by the same love he had known in the past.

> I have been down in the pit many times and I am glad to say that I have always had people who have had love and compassion, who have lifted me up and renewed my hope. Surprising how easily it's done; hope is so quickly destroyed but it can be so quickly rejuvenated. By just a touch – just by love. By that I mean, the look in somebody's eyes when they see your pain and they join your pain and just give you a hug.

In more tragic circumstances still Bishop John Robinson, author of the controversial book *Honest to God*, published in 1963, preached his last sermon in Trinity College Cambridge two months before he died of cancer. This is what he said.

> The Christian takes his stand not on optimism but on hope. This is based not on rosy prognosis but, as St Paul says, on suffering. For this, he says, trains us to endure, and endurance brings proof that we have stood the test, and this proof is the ground of hope – in the God who can bring resurrection out and through the other side of death. That is why he also says that although we carry

death with us in our bodies (all of us) we
never cease to be confident. His prayer is that
"always the greatness of Christ will shine out
clearly in my person, whether through my
life or through my death" . . . According to
my chronology he lived nearly ten years after
writing those words: others would say it was
shorter. But how little does it matter? He had
passed beyond time and its calculations. He
had risen with Christ.[2]

But we still need to ask the question: is it realistic to
go on hoping when we look around the world today?
Things surely are worse than they have ever been. It
is unsafe to walk the streets by night; there is wide-
spread unemployment; young children of eight and
nine are phoning the Samaritans because the strain
of modern life is driving them to commit suicide;
millions of people are dying of starvation the world
over; there is scarcely a country free of internal strife
or revolution, or not in dispute with another country.
And overhanging all of us is the threat of nuclear war.
How can God be in control of things if that is the
state of His creation?

Now, of course, we are all tempted to be Jeremiahs
from time to time, and imagine that human affairs
have reached such an impossible state that the only
sensible thing for God to do would be to wrap up
His creation and call it a day, and the only sensible
thing for us to do would be to lapse into cynicism
and despair. Despite all the scientific and techno-
logical progress in this century (and sometimes partly
because of this) we have seen more than our fair share
of human misery, with wars, holocausts and famine.

And Jesus Himself forecast the way in which each generation would encounter evil.

> And Jesus began to say to them, "Take heed that no one leads you astray. Many will come in my name, saying, 'I am he!' and they will lead many astray. And when you hear of wars and rumours of wars, do not be alarmed; this must take place, but the end is not yet. For nation will rise against nation, and kingdom against kingdom; there will be earthquakes in various places, there will be famines; this is but the beginning of the sufferings. But he who endures to the end will be saved."
>
> [St Mark 13:3-8, 13]

St Augustine once remarked that "you think that times past were good simply because they are not yours here and now", indicating the recurring temptation of all of us to take a dim view of our own age in comparison with any other. But if you read a history of the fourteenth century in this country, a century when the Black Death killed something like one-third of the population living between India and Iceland, you will see how in the aftermaths of the Black Death and the First World War you find the same complaints in each: economic chaos, social unrest, lower moral standards and so on. It has been said that history never repeats itself: man always does. And when we look back to the fourteenth century from the perspective of our own age, there did not seem to be much hope then of a long and happy life: indeed, just the reverse. People then never thought there was going to be a future at all. I remember how, when I was a Residentiary Canon at Manchester Cathedral, I often used to pause as I walked past a certain memorial. It records the wiping out of whole families within a few weeks or months at the time of the plague in the seventeenth century. Or just consider an age much nearer to our own time, the Victorian era, and the conditions in which most people were compelled to live their lives in this country a hundred and fifty years ago: no drinkable water, no sewers, cholera epidemics, children of seven and eight sent to work in factories and up chimneys: the list of horrors is endless.

So a little look at history ("a cordial for drooping spirits", as someone once said) gives us a much needed perspective. I find that I can more easily remember the good times in my life, and that somehow it seems as if a memory anaesthetic is blocking out the bad. And I feel that it may be just the same when we look at the world as a whole, that we forget the dark side of the world's history, and see the past as one long golden age. I checked this with Clyde Binfield, who is Reader in History at Sheffield University, the second person I interviewed in the programme.

Since the historian is honest, he will realize that the lot of most people at any given time has been anything but golden, and he has to try to display that even behind the great achievements of humankind there has been shadow, sometimes personal shadow, very often political and economic shadow too.

And he went on to say that for him

> The key point in history is an actual life
> that apparently ended on a cross; but in fact
> went through that cross into Life. Life with
> a capital "L" goes on and it is this that gives
> a perspective for me on history.

It also meant that for him, as an historian, he
could still be hopeful about the world in which
we live, even though he could never accept the
possibility of a golden age.

It was at this point that I mentioned my own
experience in Greece forty-five years ago, as an
illustration of a glimmer of hope in bad times. But
what must it be like for those in far more desperate
situations than I was in? Those, for instance, waiting
for the return of a relative who has been captured
by terrorists. Charlie Glass, an American journalist
in the Lebanon, had been kidnapped the previous
June and escaped in August. I talked to his wife,
Fiona.

> *Fiona, when Charlie was first kidnapped
> did you have very good hope that he'd be
> released very soon?*
>
> Well, there were some grounds for thinking
> that he would be released soon because he
> was kidnapped with the son of the Lebanese
> Defence Minister, who was a very prominent
> Shi-ite, and most people seemed to think that
> if he was released it would be in company
> with this guy very quickly.

But your hope was deferred?

Unfortunately, yes. They released this man and his driver after a week and they didn't release Charlie.

I think that your response to that was not to sit down and wait and hope but to take action. What did you do?

Well, initially, obviously I was more or less despairing for about a day, because I realized that he was quite likely to join the company of other hostages who've been there, some of them for years. And I thought the only way I could cope with this awful feeling was to try and do something. So I went to Washington and I spoke to people in the State Department there, to try and find out what if anything they were doing on his behalf, and I went to New York and I saw people there and finally I went to Rome to see the Pope.

What did he do for you?

Well, he was very comforting. I asked for his prayers for me and Charlie and the children and he was very compassionate. He gave me a great feeling of hope and support.

Now you have three small children. What helped to keep them cheerful?

Well, in a way, I think perhaps they helped to keep me cheerful. I suppose in order to keep their spirits up you could say I lied to them. I just told them that I was quite sure that their father would be home very soon and that there was no problem really, it was a question of waiting –

That was a sign of your own hope –

It was a sign of my own hope but it sustained me although I didn't always totally believe it. It helped to keep them going.

Now I know that Charlie's Catholic faith sustained him during his particular ordeal. What really sustained you during all that time?

It's hard to say what sustains you. Maybe hope comes more easily to people than despair.

Did any particular individual help you?

Yes, when I was in Rome a very nice priest took me on a tour of the catacombs and while we were there he pointed out the evidence of the early Christians that can still be seen in the wall-paintings, in the frescoes and in the little chapels that they had. Well, they were still being persecuted. And he said if you look carefully you see the same themes recurring again and again. People who in worldly terms you might think had no hope at all, like Jonah and the whale and Daniel in the lion's den. In each case these people were saved by God just at the last minute. So all the biblical stories came alive.

And obviously it was a tremendous support to the early Christians, which is why they kept depicting these themes because it was applicable to their own lives. He never actually said to me, "Look at this and think of your own case." But I assume that was what he meant and I did get some help.

Now, looking back over your experience, reflecting from this distance of close on six months, what do you think it has taught you, if anything, about life and hope?

I think it's taught me a lot. I think it's taught me that I was much stronger than I thought I was. When Terry Waite was first kidnapped I actually remember saying to his poor wife, I could never cope with anything like that. And then I found that I was having to cope with it even if obviously for a much shorter time than she had to. I think so many times in life you get presented with a set of circumstances and you think, "I can't bear it, I can't cope", and you do. And you come through on the other side and you feel stronger and you feel better able to maybe face the next challenge although you may not particularly look forward to it.

There is a powerful reason why Christians should never surrender to black despair. For the origin and source of our hope was born on a day when the worst in human nature seemed to triumph over all that is good. The pattern outlined on that first Good Friday, when the seeds of hope were sown just as darkness seemed to cover the world, has been repeated time and time again in human history and individual lives. And all the small experiences of hope which we derive from our ordinary everyday living are signs and symbols of the deeper hope because of what we know of Jesus Christ – not only because He rose from the dead, but also because of the way in which He died. It is a mistake to think that it was the resurrection which turned defeat into victory. The cross itself was a victory sealed by the resurrection, as the following extract from *The Healing Cross*, by a fine Presbyterian scholar, Herbert H. Farmer, earlier this century, illustrates.

Some years ago an old Polish Jew, who had been converted to the Christian faith, sat listening to a sermon by a young preacher on the love of God. And when the sermon was ended he went up to the preacher and said, "You have no right to speak of the love of God, until you have seen, as I have seen, a massacre of Jews – until you have seen, as I have seen, your parents and friends brutally murdered."

And then the preacher asked the old Jew how it was that he had come to believe in the love of God, and the Jew movingly replied that the Christian Gospel first began to lay hold of him because it bade him seek the love of God *just where he was*, just where he could not but always be, in his thoughts and memories – beside his friends in their brutal murder and execution. It bade him see the love of God not somewhere else but in the midst of just that sort of thing, in the blood and agony of Calvary. And, he went on, "As I looked at that man upon the

HOPE

cross, as I heard Him pray, Father forgive
them for they know not what they do, as I
heard Him cry in His anguish, My God,
my God, why hast Thou forsaken me, and
yet thereafter say, Father, into Thy hands
I commend my spirit, I knew I was at a
point of final crisis and decision in my life:
I knew I must make up my mind once and
for all, and either take my stand beside Him
and share in His undefeated faith in God —
or else fall finally into a bottomless pit of
bitterness, hatred and unutterable despair.[3]

I rejoice that it was in its darkest and grimmest
moments that Jesus experienced life. That gives me
real hope, because He knows what it is like to be me,
not when I am at my Sunday best, but when I am
at my Monday worst. Christian faith, that is, points
beyond tragedy to the life of victory, even in defeat;
a life of hope, even as we despair; a capacity for joy
even in sorrow. And I believe that we can have not
only hope but joy, and it is that joy that we can pass
on to others and which, like hope, the world desperately needs. Joy is not a sort of perpetual cheeriness;
indeed, in the New Testament the word "joy" occurs
in the context of suffering and separation. It was for
the joy that was set before Him that Jesus endured
the cross, and it was when He was speaking of His
own going away that He also said "no one shall
rob you of your joy". Joy is like a steady flame
which still burns in the blackest room — and joy
is born of hope. Those who are going through a
difficult patch in life are encouraged if they can
see in us that joy which is not escapist, which takes

the world's suffering seriously, and still knows that underneath "it is all right". For God is always our hope and strength . . . We can always look forward hopefully, not only because of what the past teaches, but also because of the unchanging, all-loving nature of God, our Father.

I started our second meditation by reminding viewers of a well-known newspaper photograph of twenty or more years ago, of a small naked child, with an expression of unforgettable horror on her face as she ran in terror down a street in Vietnam. She was a sort of ghastly symbol of the cruelties and barbarities of the age in which we live. There are, of course, other images which haunt us – of living skeletons in concentration camps, of starving babies in Mozambique, Ethiopia, the Sudan and elsewhere. Being constantly exposed to these images on our television screens and in our newspapers, being constantly reminded of all the injustices of human suffering in the world, how can we go on bearing it? How can those of us who live fairly secure lives remain sensitive to such scenes of suffering, without being anaesthetized by their familiarity, without being made cynical or despairing because of them?

To explore that question I talked with Barry Langridge, the Christian Aid Project Officer for India and Bangladesh. I asked him whether it didn't seem as if he was working against hopeless odds.

> Yes, it does. I mean it's bad enough when you go to a place which is new to you, and you see the poor burnt out or flooded out or in the grips of a drought and you know what's happening to them. It's even worse if

you've been working with the poor at some place for a long time, and other people have been working as well to get some fishpond or lease of land or something, and then it's all ruined and washed away after maybe ten years of work. That is much harder.

And when people make the charge about administration costs here and corruption over there?

I do a lot of talks here in the UK, and people quite rightly ask how do we know the money's getting to the right place? How do we know it's getting to the right people? And I sometimes in angrier moments feel like grabbing them by the collar and saying, "Well, how good do you want them to be?" I mean, I can tell you about a man in Bangladesh, a Bengali doctor, whom I met one day when I was on my first trip to Bangladesh and he was sitting in the evening in a very difficult part of the countryside. Then, he got out a photograph of his child. This man, a Bengali, had been educated in Russia, married a Russian girl and had come back to work in Bangladesh. He was very committed. His wife and child were still in Russia and he was waiting for them to come and he was missing his child. I was missing mine and we both had daughters of the same age and he said, "I'm waiting for them to come", and I thought, I wonder what the Russian wife will think of this place; it was a very tough place. I went back a year later; the

Russian wife had arrived, and he showed me his daughter, a beautiful child sleeping on a cot underneath a mosquito net, but the wife had had a culture shock. She was in the grips really of a breakdown I think, hated the place, thought it was dirty. She put together a rather pathetic Russian evening for us, with a glass of vodka and she made some cakes, but after that I sat with the doctor again and he said to me, "I don't think she'll last, do you?" And I said I just didn't know. I came back to England and a colleague of mine was going out a little later. I asked him to take a bottle of vodka with him. When he came back I asked if he got the bottle of vodka there, and he said, "The wife has gone back and has taken the child back to Russia". I asked about the doctor, and he said he was still there. I could not have done that. If he'd gone to Dhaka as his family wanted, gone to the capital, he could have made a nice income and kept his wife and his daughter, but he was committed to that. So when people ask me if it goes to the right people I feel like saying, "Well, come with me and I'll show you some of the right people".

You must feel depressed sometimes when you hear news of more flood and famine, so what keeps you going?

I do quite a lot of speaking in this country, and you go to a Church Hall at night and you think no one's going to turn up to hear about the Third World. Sometimes no one comes and then it's annoying as Christian Aid is not getting as much money as we hoped. But people do come and they do give, and what we like of course is when people give and when they ask interesting questions. That gives you a tremendous feeling.

So little bits of encouragement all over the place?

Yes, and I find a strong connection between people who are working hard for development in Bangladesh and people who are working hard here.

We then faced the question in another way. Is it ever right for me to enjoy a good meal because children are starving in Africa? Ought I to see the reflection of a starving child's face in every plate of food that is put in front of me? I do not share that view, and not only because I enjoy my food! It is also because our response to all the good things showered upon us should be to say "thank you" with a warm heart, and not be ungrateful. That is, we should try very hard to give to others what we so readily enjoy, as the prayer says, whilst remaining grateful for the things we enjoy . . . Of course there will always be some saintly individuals who will deny themselves in order to identify with the suffering of other people. Simone Weil, a member of the Free French movement in London during the last war, often refused food, since she was determined to eat no more than the rations in France at that time. That was right for her and some others like her, but it isn't necessarily right for all of us, and we should not allow our feelings of guilt to blot out our gratitude for the good things we are given.

As Monica Furlong says:

> Are we really forbidden to enjoy eating, and if we do, does this encourage us to feed the hungry? (How often I remember trying to forget or eliminate the friends and acquaintances who, for one reason or another, made me feel persistently guilty.) It seems to be a kind of systematic masochism. If I may never feel joyful or enjoy my bacon and eggs while anyone in the world feels hungry, then I may never feel joyful and celebrate what I am lucky enough to have. There is also a kind of arrogance implicit in the attitude, "It all depends on you". Mercifully for everyone, it doesn't all depend on me. The amount that I can take on in terms of loving or relieving the world's pain is microscopically small. A few friends, a family, a few people in really extreme forms of trouble, a sympathetic ear, small subscriptions when I pull myself together sufficiently to organize them. And I fully expect to discover as time goes on, that my little bits of love are even less effective than they feel. The times, strangely, when I have felt effective, have been the times when I have been the one in pain, or the one needing help. Or when I have had to admit, to people needing more than I could give, my own helplessness and bankruptcy of spirit.[4]

So, faced with a world men made ugly by their inhumanity, what can we do? Sometimes the problem seems so vast and the difficulties so enormous, that we are tempted to give up almost before we start – and say, "What can I possibly do to alter things?" But I have always been cheered by the historian Herbert Butterfield who, when he looked at the history of the world, said that it was always our danger to believe that if the world is going to be changed, it can only be through those people who achieve political power and do big things. The truth is, however, he went on, that the greatest contribution to the world's welfare is made by people like you and me, who do the good that lies just under our noses, and leave the leaven, as he said, to leaven the whole lump. So we can all make a practical contribution, however small, to help diminish suffering and make a better world. There are, for instance, a thousand and one ways in which we can all help in voluntary work, no matter how few gifts we think we possess. We won't delude ourselves into thinking that the voluntary organization or political party we serve is identical with the Kingdom of God, but we will perhaps recognize that if we want to work for that Kingdom, we should be ready to keep on persevering in frustrating and depressing conditions in our own community to bring the world just a little bit nearer to it. An infinitesimal contribution towards diminishing the suffering in the world, but vital too.

I then talked to Dorothy, who had been a voluntary worker for quite a long time.

There are many professional agencies which seek to diminish human suffering. What do

*you think the volunteer can offer, which per-
haps the professional can't offer?*

There's no doubt in my mind at all about
that. I think it's the opportunity to offer
time to an individual person in distress,
enough time at the right time, and certainly more time than most of the professionals
could ever hope to do. You know what it's
like: you make an appointment to go to the
doctor and you sit there in the surgery all
sort of steamed up, thinking about what
you're going to say, and you get in there
and you start off by saying apologetically,
"I don't wish to bother you, doctor, and I
know you're in a great hurry", and then you
explain what it is you have on your mind, and
when you get home you realize that several of
the things you really wanted to mention you
have completely forgotten because you know
that you've only got seven or eight minutes in
which to explain something very important.

*Are there any particular individuals who
come to your mind whom you've helped?*

The one that comes to mind first is Ruth;
she was about eighty-five, lived alone and
was very ill. In fact, she was dying, and I
called to see her in the morning and was
told the doctor had been and that he had
said that she should be admitted to hospital
but that the ambulance was probably going
to be several hours. So I stayed and I quietly
talked to her in gently reassuring terms, and
we held hands and she occasionally sipped

some water. She drifted off into sleep from time to time and she talked and she said, "I know I'm dying and I want to talk about it. I want to share this experience with somebody." That's how the day went and the ambulance then didn't come until about four o'clock in the afternoon, and I went with her in the ambulance to the hospital and saw her settled comfortably in bed. She gave me a few brief instructions as to what she wanted me to do, and then I watched her gently relax into the pillows as if she was relaxing into her dying almost. Now that was quite a time-consuming exercise, something which the professionals would never have had time to do, but I think it's very worth while.

So what does your involvement in human suffering do to you?

If I'm to be really honest I have to say that if I don't look after myself carefully it can be quite stressful. One of the difficulties is that time boundaries are not easy to arrange when you're working in a voluntary capacity. Many people in the professions have time schedules and they have a certain number of hours, and other people are responsible for their work when they are not there. But that doesn't happen when you're working in the voluntary sector. People ring you up any day of the week and sometimes during the night and you have to look after yourself. So to some extent it does mean a certain amount of pressure but something on the more positive side is undoubtedly that it makes one appreciate much more that there are many people who are suffering greatly under the surface. Often some of the people who *look* the most well are some of the people who are suffering most of all. So I think it increases one's sensitivity to other people's problems and anxieties.

So voluntary work is just one way in which we can make a contribution to a suffering world. There are, of course, other positive ways we can adopt which will nourish our human resources, make us more sensitive to human suffering and yet help us to remain firm and balanced and upright.

Not unsurprisingly, my first suggestion is to go back to the Bible. I get a bit edgy when people quote biblical texts at me, because I always suspect there are other texts which could contradict what they are telling me, and there are large parts of the Old Testament especially which often seem quite irrelevant to us today – those lists of unpronounceable names, for instance, and all those battles. And of course, the Bible has often been used for wrong ends, just as one verse from a parable of Jesus, "Compel them to come in", was used to justify all the horrors and iniquities of the Inquisition. But there are a large number of passages in both the Old and New Testaments which I find a great lift to the spirit. One writer who always encourages me is the Psalmist, because he seems to know what I am like at my worst. He often has outbursts of raging frustration and is never afraid to express his anger and to complain to God about

the injustices in the world. Just like the character in
Fiddler on the Roof, who complained to God about
poverty and illness and tiresome, awkward relatives!
But in the end the Psalmist seems to come through
and finds himself sustained by his faith that God is
in control.

> Give ear to my prayer, O God;
>> and hide not thyself from my
>> supplication.
>
> Attend to me, and answer me;
>> I am overcome by my trouble.
>
> I am distraught by the noise of the
> enemy,
>> because of the oppression of the
>> wicked.
>
> For they bring trouble upon me,
>> and in anger they cherish enmity
>> against me.
>
> My heart is in anguish within me,
>> the terrors of death have fallen upon
>> me.
>
> Fear and trembling come upon me,
>> and horror overwhelms me.
>
> And I say, "O that I had wings like
> a dove!
>> I would fly away and be at rest;
>
> yea; I would wander afar,
>> I would lodge in the wilderness.
>
> I would haste to find me a shelter
>> from the raging wind and tempest."
>
> [Psalm 55:1–8]

St Paul too had the same faith, that none of the
frustrations and pains and anxieties that we suffer
need separate us from God's love.

> For I am sure that neither death, nor life, nor
> angels, nor principalities, nor things present,
> nor things to come, nor powers, nor height,
> nor depth, nor anything else in all creation,
> will be able to separate us from the love of
> God in Christ Jesus our Lord.
>
> [Romans 8:39]

Another way for some of us to be refreshed is
through music. These days we are inundated with
music. It goes on playing and playing on the television, in the cinema, at the shops, at the office, at
work, in our living rooms, kitchens, bathrooms and
so on. On and on it plays – but somehow we are
not aware of it; it has become a sort of mechanical
background to our everyday lives. Only rarely do we
listen to it and give ourselves to it. But it is only by
listening to it, by letting it take us where it will in
spirit and imagination, that it can really do its work
in and for us.

The pianist Alfred Brendel said recently that
"music can be so many things. It can lift us into
a sphere which is remote from time and from reality."

Attending to music can make things come together, and help us to see everything in harmony. Paul
Tortelier, the great cellist, has a fascinating and
extraordinary story to tell of the way in which this
happened for him at a recital given by him and his
daughter Pau.

Pau and I gave a recital at Marlborough
College in Wiltshire on a particularly pleasant autumn evening. Already during the
Brahms E Minor Sonata, which opened the
programme, I noticed a slight shadow that
flickered from time to time across the bright-
ly lit floor. And when I began playing my
own Cello Sonata, I was aware of something
coming towards me from above, then float-
ing away again. It was there and yet not
there, like an apparition. While playing, I
had little time to give my attention to it, but
by the time I reached the middle movement
of my sonata I was able to identify my mys-
terious stage companion. It was a butterfly –
a beautifully coloured, rather big butterfly.
It began to circle around me and, as it did
so, it seemed almost to be tracing arabesques
to the music I was playing, its wings moving
in harmony with my bow. The audience's
attention had now been drawn to this whol-
ly unrehearsed ballet. Closer and closer the
butterfly would come, almost touch me, and
then fly away. It was having a flirtation with
me, or perhaps I with it. The slow movement
of my sonata concludes quietly on a sustained
harmonic. At that moment I closed my eyes,
my bow barely moving on the string. I did
not want to disturb the atmosphere of peace
and calm. As I slowly drew the note to an end
I opened my eyes again, and there, perched
on my left hand, was the butterfly. It had
alighted so gently that I hadn't even felt its
presence. For a moment or two we looked

at each other. It didn't move; I didn't move. It was so lovely, so ethereal that I couldn't bring myself to shake it off. It had chosen the ideal moment for repose, I thought, settling there at the end of the slow movement; it seemed not to want to fly away. What could I do? Almost without thinking, I slowly brought my hand, with the butterfly still perched on it, up to my lips. I was sure it would fly away, but it didn't. I kissed it very tenderly, but it still didn't move. Not everyone has been able to kiss a butterfly. I never thought I would do so, least of all on the concert stage. Finally I shook my hand very gently and it floated off into the air. That was just before the interval. After the interval we played Beethoven's A Major Sonata, and there was the butterfly again dancing all the way through, only coming down to rest from time to time on Pau's music as if wanting to have a look at what she was doing. The piece came to an end and the butterfly was nowhere to be seen. "Aha", I thought, "it has left us to join the other butterflies in the fields." Not at all. It was perched on my foot, and as the audience applauded it flapped its wings.

Who can judge what forces of spirit or nature guide our actions and bring harmony to seemingly disparate things? Such forces are there; that's all I need to know. The audience that day knew it also. We had all lived a fairy tale.[5]

Some of us will find help and inspiration in poetry, through caring for pets, fishing, bird-watching, looking at scenes of nature and so on – all according to our temperament and opportunities. I have always thought it important to have a hobby, right away from our work and main concerns, which we pursue just for its own sake. What is important all the time is that we don't let the things of the moment, and especially bad news, overwhelm us and that we give ourselves space to stand back, put ourselves and our everyday affairs in a larger context. The odd thing is that when we do, we attend to those affairs better, and with a larger sensitivity than we had before, because we are seeing them with fresher eyes, eyes that aren't jaded by over-familiar perceptions. Anthony Fry, a psychiatrist, has recently written a book called *Safe Space*,[6] in which he argues that we all need that space if we are going to function well in life. He was the person I talked to next.

What do you mean by this phrase "Safe Space"?

Well, "Safe Space" is really first and foremost the absence of any gross physical threat. Secondly, it involves some sense that you are in a space where you feel all right about yourself and thirdly, some kind of linkage with other people, some sense of belonging or if not with other people, with something. Some sense of being there, being in the right place.

Well now, suppose that I actually live in an overcrowded apartment in a tower block in

149

*the city of Liverpool or somewhere like it, how
can I ensure this "Safe Space" for myself?*

It's not an easy thing to find, and "Safe
Space" is about both your material environment and your personal environment.
Try and find some little bit of your flat or
some surrounding park or somewhere where
you feel a sense of peace, where you feel at
ease, and also make sure that at least some
of your personal relationships make you feel
sustained and contained and make you feel
safe.

*What do you regard as the most important
component of this safe space?*

If I was left with one element which con-
tributes to human safety and which I as
a psychiatrist have seen in my practice, I
would say it is being linked to other people
or being loved by other people or being cared
for. That to me is the most important component of the sense of safety. Without that
it's very difficult to feel safe.

*Do you think that God or religion has any-
thing to do with the safe space? I noticed that
in your book you say the God without must
come alive as the God within. What do you
mean by that?*

I feel very much that many religions are
striving after some sense of continuity and
purpose and belonging, and all through religious thought there is an idea that this
transcends the boundaries of the individual

person and also transcends time, and that this linkage with those who went before and those who will come after is a very important part of our belonging and feeling safe.

Knowing all that you know about this threatening environment in which we all live, are you still hopeful about people and about the age in which we live?

Well, I've been in an inner city psychiatric practice for eleven years now and I've seen people come through the most terrible things, and somehow human fortitude and ingenuity I think in the long run will save us and so, yes, I am hopeful.

Talking of a safe space, I am not very good at remembering poetry, but one verse I learnt for a school examination years ago has stayed with me all these years. It is by Matthew Arnold:

> Calm soul of all things
> Make it mine
> To feel amid the city's jar
> That there abides a peace of thine
> Man did not make and cannot mar.

I think we need to hang on to this, that in the midst of our busiest and most frantic moments, that inner peace is still possible and that when we are aware of that inner peace, there are many things we shall begin to see which we have never noticed before.

John Taylor has a true story which illustrates this well.

A young married man who worked at Heath-row Airport told me once how he and his wife had taken their two children for a day at the seaside. Their little boy of eighteen months needed the public toilet, and the father set out with him to cross the rough unmetalled road above the beach. The expedition lasted all of half an hour, he told me, because every pebble, every bit of shell, every dry twig on the surface of that road was an object of such wonder that they had to squat and examine and exclaim. Heaven lies about us in our infancy, and even a visit to the loo can become the golden journey to Samarkand. Where did it go, that intensity of response? How comes it that most of us lose the gift of seeing the ordinary as extraordinary? This is why Jesus Christ said that the Kingdom of God is for the childlike, for it is the kingdom of the fully alive. The unaware and the half-dead have no place in it because they have no feeling for it.

On the other hand, those who welcome life with all its ambiguity and are kept open to the flow and exchange of that life, seem able to come to terms with their mortality almost as a matter of small account. There is a lovely example of this in a prayer composed by an Oxford undergraduate a few days after the outbreak of the First World War, in which he was to be killed three years later. It runs:

To have given me self-consciousness but for an hour in a world so breathless with beauty would have been enough. But Thou hast preserved it within me for twenty years now and more, and hast crowned it with the joy of this summer of summers. And so, come what may, whether life or death, and, if death, whether bliss unimaginable or nothingness, I thank Thee and bless Thy name.[7]

Another way in which people are sustained every day is through meditation. We offered viewers a leaflet describing three simple ways to meditate, and this is reproduced in an Appendix.

Many meditators are in quest of truth, wisdom, ultimate values – things they have failed to find within their own religious tradition. It could be plausibly argued that secular meditation has arisen partly because traditional and established religion has ceased to give people, particularly young people, the religious experience for which they are craving. So they look elsewhere. They are tired of dogmas and formulations and words – "Words, words, words!" said Hamlet. However necessary these formulations may be (and some formulation is, I believe, necessary), they can sometimes erect barriers between man and reality. And contemporary man wants reality; he wants experience; he wants practice; he wants a "way". Way or *tao*, the great Eastern word used to describe religious experience, appears frequently in the Old Testament, and Christians were called "followers of the way", just as their founder called Himself the Way. Anyhow, experience of meditation gives people the sense of being on a way that goes somewhere; and that is what they want.[8]

Meditation comes in different forms — religious and non-religious — and is found by many to be of great value in their search for inner peace.

There is one way of being sustained which is open to us all. Have you ever thought how important silence is in our lives? I am afraid the truth is that because of our chattiness we often become afraid of silence. I have noticed how anxious people can become when they are asked to keep silence for a few minutes, as if they have only got one thought in their head — when will this be over? And I can recall how as a child the two minutes' silence of Armistice seemed to go on for hours — but these words put a different complexion on the matter.

In our chatty world, in which the word has lost its power to communicate, silence helps us to keep our mind and heart anchored in the future world and allows us to speak from there a creative and recreative word to the present world. Thus silence can also give us concrete guidance.

Too often our words are superfluous, inauthentic, and shallow. It is a good discipline to wonder in each new situation if people wouldn't be better served by our silence than by our words. But having acknowledged this, a more important message is that silence is above all a quality of the heart that can stay with us even in our conversation with others. It is a portable cell that we carry with us wherever we go. From it we speak to those in need and to it we return after our words have borne fruit.

It is in this portable cell that we find ourselves immersed in divine silence. The final question concerning our silence is not whether we say much or little, but whether our words call forth the caring silence of God Himself. It is to this silence that we are all called: words are the instrument of the present world, but silence is the mystery of the future world.[9]

So we concluded the meditation sharing some silence together.

Our third and last meditation of this series turned back to ourselves and asked what sort of hope there was for us as human beings, that we would grow in maturity as we were meant to?

By now it was 17th January – how many New Year Resolutions still existed? But New Year Resolutions, I am convinced, point to something deep inside of us: the desire to be better people than we were. This instinct for goodness was illustrated by the novelist and philosopher Iris Murdoch in an interview she had on Border Television:

I believe in good as something which arises in the soul. It's something which each person is able to recognize. I think people sometimes

profess to be "beyond good and evil" or to
be so cynical that they don't see any difference; but this is just play acting. They
are wanting to dissociate themselves from a
particular version of the distinction. But the
difference I think lives with us all. In this
sense I believe that the reality of good is
connected with the reality of all our strivings
– it's something we come across every day in
all the things we do, how we employ our time
and how we think about people, whether we
are able to learn difficult things and really
care about other people, or whether we're
selfish and satisfied with what is superficial.
All the struggles that happen in the process
of being a human being are connected with
the reality of the struggle between good and
evil, and the connection of good with the
genuine, with what's true.[10]

So goodness, Iris Murdoch is saying, is not something that happens in a rarified spiritual atmosphere
unconnected with everyday living, but is very much
connected with our ordinary lives, confused and
messy as they sometimes are. There is no short
cut to goodness. Our growth in goodness will be
slow and painful, and sometimes we won't seem
to be making any progress at all. Sometimes, too,
it will show itself in the most unlikely people and
in the most unlikely ways.

I then introduced Father Hilary. He is a rather
unusual combination, because as well as being a
member of a monastic order, with all its emphasis
on prayer and discipline, he is also an inner city

parish priest. And that means that he is daily in touch with people whose lives are spoilt by poverty, unemployment, vandalism and ugliness.

Hilary, on the surface there wouldn't seem to be much in common between a monk who withdraws from the world and an inner city parish priest who has to be active in a deprived environment, so how do you see the link between the two?

Well, I think a religious community is, at least mine is, a gathering together of very ordinary simple human beings from mixed backgrounds and so on, and they have to grow together in a community of love by tolerating each other, understanding each other and eventually forgiving each other. And one suddenly discovers that really that same sort of thing is happening and should be happening in anywhere you find yourself living, so there is no real difference between a community in the sense of a religious community and the people around you in the suburbs or wherever you are.

So from your experience are you still hopeful that people have this instinct for goodness even when they're living in conditions of perhaps poverty and squalor?

Yes. I think I'm very impressed by the way in which all sorts of people who wouldn't claim to be religious or to be churchgoers or anything like that have a deep desire to find goodness, particularly in people who've died. It's a very, very common thing for somebody who's grieving a death to say of her husband, for instance, that he was a very good man *really*. And I can remember one very striking story. A woman had lost her sister very suddenly with a brain tumour, and unfortunately the last encounter she'd had with her sister was a row. There'd been a shouting match. So she went to the funeral parlour to see the body of her dead sister and begged forgiveness, and then came to me and said, "Father, she did hear me, didn't she, and she did forgive me?" And I think this very poignant thing showed me that in everybody there is a yearning to be approved of, to be accepted by God, and this can only come through other people.

So what do you think is the most important element in our growth toward this goodness?

Loving the people that we live and work with. Certainly in the early Church, observers said, See how these Christians love each other! It may have been sarcasm, but it certainly applies today that any effectiveness that the Church has will come out of the way in which the members forgive and love each other.

Hilary, how do you see this goodness of which we're speaking developing in yourself as a monk and as a parish priest?

I can't. All I can see is people putting up with me and forgiving me and accepting me. I suppose they do more and more of it

158

as I go on, but I'm the last person to see anything improving in myself.

Of course, as Hilary hinted, when we talk about being good, or being better, we are not talking about being perfect: we are talking about risk, uncertainty, the courage to stand out against whatever people think. Goodness is not conforming to a rule or role; it is not a matter of reacting to things but a matter of acting creatively, the fruit of the imagination. So it becomes the expression of super-abundant life. It is our way of becoming more and more what we are, so that other people may be enabled to do the same. And the key, of course, is love, the increasing, extending and deepening of our love for other people because they are loved by God themselves.

> Love is patient; love is kind and envies no one. Love is never boastful, nor conceited, nor rude; never selfish; not quick to take offence. Love keeps no score of wrongs; does not gloat over other men's sins, but delights in the truth. There is nothing love cannot face; there is no limit to its faith, its hope, and its endurance.

Such love can't be regimented, it shows itself in a thousand different ways for each one of us; it is always spontaneous; it never seeks either praise or reward, and it's the secret of all goodness.

I quoted the example of an everyday incident in the hope that it would help us to see that if only we would let go, and respond to such incidents in the spirit of gay abandon, they contain unexpected joy.

Consider, for instance, what happened to Bill Holt. When he was sixty years of age Bill was one day walking up a cobbled street in the town of Todmorden, which lies in the Pennine Hills of northern England. Also on the street was a rag-and-bone man with his horse and cart; the horse was skinny and ill-cared-for, and the man was treating it badly. Bill was moved at the sight of the horse and protested to the rag-and-bone man. "What's it got to do with you?" the man answered. "Anyway, if you're that concerned about it, you can have it for five pounds." Bill, of course, had no need for a horse; but in a spirit of abandon he said, "All right, I'll have it." So he paid five pounds, which he could ill afford, for a horse of which he had no need. And it changed his life. He gave the horse a name; he called it Trigger. And once he had fed it up on the land around his cottage, and the two of them, horse and man, had learnt to sleep outdoors together, their bodies warming each other, they set out on a pilgrimage together all over Europe. They travelled through France and Italy and Spain, Austria, Germany and the Netherlands. Most often, when evening came, they would ask a friendly farmer to allow them to stay in the corner of one of his fields; Trigger would lie down and Bill would curl up against his belly. Already a naturally religious person, though not by temperament orthodox, Bill's religious sense deepened tremendously during his years of pilgrimage with Trigger. And who can doubt that his unexpected joy was all contained within that moment of grace when God called to him through a skinny horse and he responded so hilariously?

Every event of daily life can serve as spiritual exercise. And everything can serve as your guru, your teacher, if only you will attend to it – even a skinny horse.[11]

What I love about that story is Bill's recklessness in buying Trigger. I love the way in which quite spontaneously he responds to the rag-and-bone man, because to me it is being spontaneous, the overflowing of a loving heart, which is a mark of true goodness.

Spontaneous goodness is the fruit of the heart, and that means staying close to the source of all goodness. That which continually spoils our efforts at being better, our growth and goodness, is the way in which self always gets in the way. But the more we contemplate God and His love, the more we are put into a proper perspective, the more unconsciously we grow in goodness, and the better we are.

So we were led back finally in our prayers to Jesus Himself. As Father Michael Child put it:

Jesus said, "Come to me all of you who labour and are overburdened; and I will give you rest. Shoulder my yoke and learn from me for I am gentle and humble in heart, and you will find rest for your souls. Yes, my yoke is easy and my burden light."

The Christmas story reminds us of the humility and gentleness of Jesus. God's word was made flesh in an obscure country in lowly circumstances. God's word comes to us with discretion and humility. Some of us believe, others go away disappointed. If we respond humbly to His humble invitation, we follow Him also in His ministry of healing and forgiving. Openness to others makes us vulnerable. Sharing the love of Jesus for all men and women will lead us to suffering and perhaps death.

But the disciple is not greater than the Master and we will suffer, as He told us He would.

When Jesus told Peter to walk towards Him on the lake, Peter stayed afloat as long as his eyes were fixed on Jesus. But when he looks at the wind and the waves and loses sight of Jesus, he sinks beneath the waves.

We may be unfaithful and sleep while Jesus is in agony in the garden of Gethsemane.

We may run away from the crucifixion at Calvary, but He will rejoin us on the road to Emmaus after God has raised Him from the dead.

He is with us on our journey now. We may not recognize Him, but neither did the disciples. But their hearts were open. They talked to Him, shared their hopes and thoughts and invited Him to join them for a meal.

Then they recognized Him in the breaking

of bread.

This experience transformed them, and by the power of the Spirit hope and joy and power were let loose into our world. And God will wipe away all tears from our eyes; there will be no more mourning or sadness. There is a new creation.

The pastoral care support system we offered after this series of meditations was similar to that after previous meditations – but with one major difference. Instead of using Family Care Line counsellors, who had served us well in the past, we recruited our own body of counsellors. There were those who already worked for voluntary counselling agencies as Christians, and those whom I had helped to train over the past twenty years in the University extra-mural courses I had taught. Notice that I say "*as* Christians". I am always hesitant to use the phrase "Christian counsellor" because to many people it suggests that the counsellor will not be completely open or unconditional in his counselling, and may seek to "use" the occasion for evangelistic purposes.

We used British Telecom's Link Line service, enabling viewers nationwide to dial at the cost of a local call, and we had eighteen counsellors servicing fifteen lines. The lines were open for two hours after each meditation, but on every occasion, some counsellors were phoning viewers back with calls that went on for a considerable time after the two hours had elapsed. British Telecom monitored the number of calls, and whilst the average number we were able to handle was around 230, the average number of callers trying to reach us was something like 1,150. This, I fear, represented both success and failure on our part. Success in that the meditations had achieved what we were hoping they would achieve: they spoke to people where they were, and elicited such confidence that so many people were prepared to ask for help. Failure in that we had raised expectations of help, and had only been able to deal with such a limited number of requests. Our only plea in defence would be that where viewers were unable to contact us by phone, they were able to write – and write they did, in great numbers!

It was as clear from our correspondence as from the phone calls that we had hit on the most appropriate subject for the start of the year, and it was greatly encouraging to read, for instance, that many people suffering bereavement, unemployment, seemingly incurable illness and the like had felt fresh stirrings of hope. Perhaps one viewer from Essex, more than any other, illustrated this when he wrote, "I never thought it possible for television to *inspire* me as your programmes have done. I'm used to it giving me a way of escape or putting me to sleep when I come home from work. But you've given me real food for reflection, and I can now look on this new year, with all the difficulties (especially of family troubles) that I face, with a new heart . . . And you've made Christian faith real to me . . ."

We were able to make personal contacts (largely, again, thanks to the availability and willingness of local churches) for about seventy-four people. Having made those contacts, we leave it to those in the region in which the viewer lives to deal with the situation as their resources allow, and without any

interference from us. Occasionally (and this heart-
ens us) they let us know how they have been able
to help. We have sometimes wondered whether we
should attempt some sort of monitoring, to discover
how effectively help is given. But we prefer reticence
and trust in such delicate, personal operations. The
present mania for analysis and research can be taken
too far – and has little place, I believe, in matters
pastoral.

Several of our counsellors revealed afterwards
that their feeling was not primarily a feeling of
satisfaction at work well done, but an overwhelm-
ing feeling of frustration or sometimes failure, in
dealing with situations that appeared to be well-nigh
intractable. A single parent trying to cope with a
mentally-handicapped child and alcoholic parents;
a desperately lonely woman, who had been sexually
abused as a child, and unable to tell anyone about
it until that morning; a man in his late seventies,
friendless, because of his self-confessed "bloody-
mindedness" . . . It seemed to many of us as if we
had only been able to put one toe into an ocean of
turbulent and inexhaustible need. Yet even that, we
felt, is better than simply surveying the scene with
pity from the safety of the shore.

CHAPTER ELEVEN

Retrospect and Prospect

Perhaps it's necessary as this book draws to a close to make a disclaimer! I have told in some ways a very personal story, the story of the way in which Air Care has been for me some sort of climax in a lifetime concerned with and committed to pastoral care. But essentially, the whole experiment is the fruit of many people's devotion and labours: the encouragement of Executive Producers, the team-work of the Advisers, Producer and Director, the tireless efforts of members of the film crew to "get things right" . . .

A disclaimer, too, perhaps, of another sort. A tendency to self-importance, perhaps, is the beset-ting sin of the television world; and lest it be thought that we delude ourselves about the importance of the experiment in which we have been engaged, it is necessary to stress again our limited servant role in it all. So far, for instance, as making contacts for people, we have done no more than act as a sort of clearing-house; so far as our counsellors have spent valuable time in listening to people in the limited and difficult operation that telephone-counselling is, they have only done (as they are the first to admit) what many other counsellors have done in similar circumstances.

Nevertheless, perhaps we can modestly claim something of a breakthrough in the world of religious broadcasting. In his book, *God-in-a-Box*, Colin Morris, formerly Head of Religious Broadcasting at the BBC, claims that:

> By courtesy of mass media, we Christian communicators can tell the whole world about the love of God without its costing us anything more than the expenditure of a little technique and a lot of breath. It is love at a distance; at the other end of the microphone, camera or printing press. No one can tap us on the shoulder and say, "Prove it!" We are beyond reach.[1]

We have tried, however inadequately, to put ourselves within reach by taking seriously the troubles of those to whom we speak. We have tried to diminish the distance at which Colin Morris says our love is exercised. And our venture has certainly cost a lot of people more than "the expenditure of a little technique and a lot of breath". It has called out a deal of self-sacrifice in response to perceived human need, the sort of response that pastoral care always involves.

Of course, there is always an inherent contradiction in the use of the mass media for the purposes of religion. We are always, as Colin Morris says, "trying to proclaim from a position of immense secular power the futility of secular power compared to the divine strength exhibited in utter weakness on the Cross. We are like a millionaire preaching the virtue of poverty from the back seat of a gold-plated Rolls."[2]

If that colourful image cuts us down to size, it is, at the same time, no excuse for not using this powerful medium to make contact with and serve the needs of real people, so far as all the limitations allow. And further, if our role is but a humble, servant role, it is establishing a bridgehead with the life of the local church, a bridgehead which has been glaringly absent in the history of religious television. Time and time again in talking with church groups, I have discovered how little time and attention has been given to this whole field – and the fault lies on both sides. We on our side have not done nearly enough to make the connection. We can only claim that at a late hour, we have been trying to build that bridgehead, not through talk, but through mutual co-operative service to those in need.

And what of the future? We plan more Meditations, and must ensure that we have more telephone lines and more counsellors, so that we are in no danger of creating expectations which we cannot fulfil. But we work at a time when all public service broadcasting is under threat, and all the pressures are for us to pursue the road labelled "down-market". Yet pressures represent challenge. And the challenge to us is to produce, and go on producing, religious programmes which are not merely interesting documentaries on what is happening in the religious life of today; or social, political and economic critiques; or bland soporifics, simply appealing to conservative and old-fashioned instincts. The reason why so many people turn their back on traditional Christianity is because it seems to them massively irrelevant in their own personal lives. As Cyprian Smith put it,

Does what I hear from the pulpit, or read in religious books, have any connection at all with life as I actually live it, with the sort of person I am in the deepest or most secret core of myself? What use is it to me to be told that I am "redeemed" or "saved" by Christ, when all I find within myself is a frothing cauldron of conflicting desires, fears and insecurities?[3]

It is to that "deepest or most secret core", that "frothing cauldron of conflicting desires, fears and insecurities" that we try to address ourselves in our meditations, and enable expression to be given in our Air Care system. The more we bite into ordinary consciousness, the more we shall deserve to be heard – and the more, too, we will be unable to be ignored. It isn't, in other words, political sense and religious pressure groups which will ensure the survival of religious programming: it is their *worth*, sheer *worth*.

EPILOGUE

Curiouser and Curiouser . . .

Perhaps it's a certain restlessness of spirit in me
that hates to leave ends untied, and has prompted
two recent return visits to Greece.

I had always wondered what happened to the
pilot and navigator of the third aircraft behind us
in that fateful raid in August 1943, the aircraft we
saw burning as we waited to be picked up from
the water. Were they buried and if so, where? I
returned to Preveza to try to find out, and another
amazing coincidence occurred. After several abortive
attempts to solve the mystery, I happened to meet
two fishermen toiling up a hill outside the town as
they returned from their day's catch. As I told them
my story by means of bizarre signs and gestures,
since my inability to speak modern Greek is almost
total, I could see the dawning of recognition on their
faces. Excitedly, they made me understand that as
teenagers they had actually seen the raid from the
shore, and could remember exactly the spot where
we came down in the water and where number three
spun in on land. They were able to take me to the
site, a derelict piece of ground, and explained that
the heat of the day and the heat of the fire were
so intense that there were few remains. (I have
since discovered that they were both buried in the

Phaleron War Cemetery in Athens.) The memory of those two happy characters and their sudden extinction lingered vividly; and the haunting, agonizing, unanswerable question which has tormented so many survivors raised its head: Why them, not us? Why him, not me?

But there was another loose end to be tied, another story not quite finished. The Greek girl who had bravely stepped from the pavement in 1943, and who had heard me recount the incident in the first of our Meditations on Hope: we had to meet to complete the story. Our reunion forty-five years after our first encounter was celebrated in a restaurant in a suburb of Athens when eight of us sat down to a splendid meal. It was, to say the least, an emotional evening, especially for the two main participants. As we lovingly looked back on the story, more details emerged which made it even more curious. Significantly, in 1943 our Greek girl had left school and just started working for the International Red Cross, the organization which played such a large part in making our lives as prisoners much less miserable than they might have been. But what seemed extraordinary was the accidental or providential way in which she saw the Meditations at all. Usually, while staying with her daughter, she goes to the Greek Orthodox Church on Sunday morning. She had been prevented that morning, since her great friend was due to fly back to Greece later that day. So they switched the television on and were watching a programme on Japanese finance on Channel 4 at the time of the Meditation. Since my friend was forced to vacate the room she went to another one, and switched on the television, turning from Channel 1 to Channel

2 to Channel 3 before she got to Channel 4. When she arrived at Channel 3 she saw my face, and four seconds later heard me recount the story of her generous act. Her friend told me that she staggered out of the room white and trembling, spending most of the rest of the day in tears. Her friend also pointed out that the night before the broadcast, they had been to Covent Garden with a twenty pound ticket going spare. They were approached by a lady who was without a ticket but who couldn't afford twenty pounds. And so, with the same impulsive greatness of heart that she had displayed exactly forty-five years previously to a complete stranger, my Greek friend handed over the ticket . . .

There is only one small area of disagreement about that first meeting of ours. Although my Greek friend thinks that her gift was of cigarettes, I still maintain that it was a packet of sweets. But what matter? The whole story to me is a superb illustration of the ripples caused by one small spontaneous act of generosity prompted by real caring for others whoever they are, or in whatever circumstances they find themselves. So whilst this is the end of this particular story, in another sense the story never ends. . .

APPENDIX

~~~~~~~~

Simple Ways to Meditate

Meditation often seems to be a frightening exercise, demanding complicated techniques and a highly-developed religious sense. But think of it SIMPLY: it is a way of calming our restless hearts and minds, a way (if we persevere) to find inner peace.

Here are one or two different ways, which you may find helpful. Choose that which best suits your background and religious tradition – or lack of it!

I THE "MANTRA" WAY

1 Adopt a comfortable sitting position, in which you can feel completely relaxed.

2 Fix on one word which doesn't necessarily have any particular meaning, since it is the sound that matters, and not the meaning. (The purpose is to *prevent* rather than *encourage* thought.) This is sometimes known as your "Mantra", and a well-known Mantra is the Indian *OM*, some Christians find it more helpful to use "Jesus" or "God". What matters is that you repeat the Mantra passively, without being diverted into mental reflection.

At first you may find that ten minutes is as much concentration as you can manage, but you should be able to increase that after a time without too much difficulty. The ideal, of course, is twenty minutes in the morning, and twenty minutes in the evening.

II THE "CONTEMPLATIVE" WAY

1 Again, adopt a comfortable sitting and relaxed position.

2 Fix on one natural object – a flower, a plant, a tree – or a picture or a cross – for five to ten minutes, and simply contemplate it. Absorb it, and be absorbed into it, without involving yourself in any mental activity concerning it.

Those who practise this way tell how, when saying prayers has become a lifeless exercise for them, they have been renewed and become much more aware of and alive to the world around them. (Remember Jesus's words about "opening the eyes of the blind"? A lot of spiritual and human growth depends on our ability properly to "see".)

III THE "GOSPEL" WAY

1 Choose a scene from the gospels such as the Feeding of the Five Thousand. Imagine as vividly as you can the scene: the hungry crowd, the anxious disciples, the boy with the loaves and fishes, and Jesus, unhurried and untroubled, "in the midst". Imagine yourself as one of the crowd, or close to the physical presence of Jesus. What would be your impression of Him? What would you want to do after you have been fed?

2 This will lead you on to consider: a) how you are fed now both materially and spiritually, and lead you to thanksgiving in your prayer;

b) the starvation in the Third World, and to ask God's blessing on all agencies designed to help.

You can repeat this method many times with different stories from the gospels. Its importance lies in the way it brings you close to the Presence of Jesus – and "keeping company" with Him is an essential in motivating our faith.

I have deliberately suggested simple ways and I hope that you will find at least one of them a help. There are always more advanced ways later on!

Notes and Acknowledgements

The author acknowledges with gratitude his debt to all the people whose work has helped him, and especially to those listed here.

Prologue
1 Arthur Miller, *Timebends*, Methuen 1987, pp.134-5

Chapter One
1 George Orwell, *The Road to Wigan Pier*, Victor Gollancz 1937
2 Charles Morgan, *The Fountain* and *Sparkenbroke*, Macmillan
3 John MacMurray, *Reason and Emotion*, Faber

Chapter Two
1 Frank Wright, *Exploration into Goodness*, S.C.M. Press 1988, Ch. 7.

Chapter Three
1 William Temple, *Christianity and the Social Order*, Penguin

Chapter Four
1 Frank Wright, *Pastoral Care for Lay People*, S.C.M. Press 1982, Ch. 1.

Chapter Five

1   R. M. Hare in *Aims in Education*, ed. T. H. B. Hollins, Manchester University Press 1964, pp. 69-70

Chapter Six

1   Kenneth Clark, *Civilization*, BBC/John Murray 1969, p. xvi

Chapter Seven

1   Quoted in Peter Heinze, *Air Care*, World Association for Christian Communication 1982

Chapter Eight

1   Quoted Glebsch & Jaeckle, *Pastoral Care in Historical Perspective*, Harper Torch Books, New York 1967, pp. 127-8

2   Henri Nouwen, *Letter of Consolation*, Gill & Macmillan 1983, pp. 81-2

3   Christine Smith, *Clouds Got in my Way*, Eyre Methuen 1981

4   Dietrich Bonhoeffer, *Letters and Papers from Prison*, S.C.M. Press 1953, p. 183

5   George Herbert, *Love bade me Welcome*

6   John Donne, *Wilt thou forgive. . .?*

7   H. W. Longfellow, *It is too late*!

8   Glin Bennett, *Patients and Their Doctors*, Balliers Tindell 1979, p. 129

9   Henry Scott Holland (1847-1918)

10 Bede Jarrett (source unknown)

11   Harry Williams, *True Resurrection*, Mitchell Beazley 1972, and Fount Paperbacks 1983, pp. 180-1

Chapter Nine

1   J. B. Priestley, *Delight*, Heinemann, 1949, pp. 101-2

2   Joyce Grenfell, *Joyce Grenfell Requests the Pleasure*, Futura Publications 1977

3   *Collected Poems of Wilfred Owen*, Ed. C. Day Lewis, Chatto & Windus 1968, p. 44

4   David Tinker, *A Message from the Falklands*, Penguin 1983

5   J. Gillespie Magee, Jr., original manuscript in the Library of Congress at Washington, U.S.A.

6   L. Charles Birch, *Nature and God*, S.C.M. Press 1965, pp. 123-4

7   Norman Pittenger, *Picturing God*, S.C.M. Press 1982, p. 124

8   Ed. George Appleton, *Oxford Book of Prayer*, O.U.P. 1985, p. 367

9   John Wesley's Diary

10   *Oxford Book of Prayers*, O.U.P. 1985, pp. 458-9

Chapter Ten

1   *Complete Poems of Emily Dickinson*, Ed. T. H. Johnson, Faber 1975, p. 116

2   John A. T. Robinson, *Where Three Ways Meet*, S.C.M. Press 1987, p. 194

3   H. H. Farmer, *The Healing Cross*, Nisbet

4   Monica Furlong, *Travelling In*, Hodder & Stoughton 1971, p. 80

5   Paul Tortelier, *Paul Tortelier*, Heinemann, pp. 144-5

6   Anthony Fry, *Safe Space*, Dent 1987

7   J. V. Taylor, *A Matter of Life and Death*, S.C.M. Press 1986, pp. 20 and 28

8   William Johnston, *Silent Music*, Collins 1974, p. 219

9   Henri Nouwen, *The Way of the Heart*, Darton, Longman & Todd 1981, p. 65

10   Iris Murdoch, *Revelations*, Shepheard-Welwyn 1985, p. 85

11   Donald Nicholl, *Holiness*, Darton, Longman & Todd 1981, p. 109

Chapter Eleven
1   Colin Morris, *God-in-a-Box*, Hodder & Stoughton 1984, p. 229

2   Ibid., p. 230

3   *The Times*, 11th June 1988